The Riddle of One Samuel

A Personal Reading of the Hebrew Text

By David F Pennant

David Pennant

1.1.24

Silver Lining Books

Woking

The Riddle of One Samuel

copyright © David F Pennant 2024

ISBN 978-1-7392029-4-1

Cover photo: Psalm 19. Sunset at Margate, Kent on 8.10.23.

Published by Silver Lining Books

30 Oriental Road, Woking, Surrey, GU22 7AW

www.pennantpublishing.co.uk

Contents

Foreword

In 1981 I enrolled at Trinity College Bristol as a candidate for ordination in the Church of England. I was keen to read the Bible in the original tongues. After a couple of years, my Hebrew tutor suggested I might like to do some research before taking a post in the church because I showed aptitude in the language. One of my set texts for the London BD degree which I was following was the story of Samson in Judges chapters thirteen to sixteen. For my study, I looked at wordplay in the whole book of Judges.

I had noticed several kinds of literary subtlety; what I called rootplay, repeated words which I called Leading Words, plays on the names of characters, and links to earlier parts of Israel's story in the Hebrew Bible. My method was to read through the book of Judges in the Hebrew twenty times, noting down my findings. Then it was a case of seeing whether other people had come up with similar observations. I spent two years reading scholarly books and articles and discovered that my insights were genuinely new. I wrote up my work and was awarded a PhD (1). I had found the research enormously enjoyable.

סֶ יֶ סֶ רֶ אַ   שׁ מִי כָ ה

Samek   Sounds like Samek

Interpreting my findings was not straightforward. While it was a fact that the enemy general SYSRA or Sisera as we spell him (the word on the right) had two Sameks in his name and he was hidden by Jael the Kenite under a SaMYKaH or covering (the word on the left), the significance of this was hard to come by (2). Was the similarity between the letter name of the two Sameks and the sound of the word SaMYKaH coincidental? If the choice of the word SaMYKaH was a deliberate play on the letters in Sisera's name, what was its purpose? Might it be no more than a literary device to hold the reader's attention, and perhaps solicit a smile, rather like the puns in our national press beloved of headline writers? What was I to make of it?

שׁ שׂ צ ס
sh   s   s   s

Non-Hebraists, read from right to left. Please note that there are not just two but three letters in the Hebrew alphabet with S sounds, or four if you distinguish between the two versions of Sin / Shin. I transliterate them all with our letter S. Confusing?

You bet. Sorry. Note also that written Hebrew has the consonants only. I will occasionally add vowels in transliteration if I think it is helpful, mostly to aid pronunciation. My advice is to take very little notice of the vowels. Finally, I use 3 to transliterate Ayin. More confused than ever? Naturally.

In passing, players of the board game Monopoly might wryly observe that when it came to the crunch, Sisera did not have a get out of Jael free card. (Do not pass GO! Do not collect £200!). Jael's tent of welcome was not to be confused with a rent-free hotel. There was a price to pay.

Alternatively, might there be some greater significance to the Sisera – Samek connection? Could an awareness of this and other proposed literary devices contribute to a deeper understanding of the book?

Some thirty-five years later, at the urging of my online Hebrew student Richard Bicknell, I have extended my enquiry into One Samuel, the next part of Israel's story. The similarities between Samson and Samuel have long impressed me – both were born to previously barren women, both were Nazirites from birth, and both became judges leading the nation in opposition to the ever present and hostile Philistines (3). This similarity encouraged me to see the continuing story as a whole. Might there be literary devices in One Samuel like the ones I had discerned in Judges to unearth and consider?

My method has been the same as in my earlier research. I have reflected carefully on the Hebrew text, noted what emerged and pondered. I have tried to write in a way that makes this book accessible to non-Hebraists as well as people who read the Bible in the original language by explaining everything carefully with the use of diagrams.

As for checking whether others have seen and commented on the matters I propose, there are several recent studies of what I call rootplay in the Bible text. Chief of these is the work of Isaac Kalimi; a reviewer declared that his book *Metathesis in the Hebrew Bible* was likely to become the standard work for several decades to come (4).

Scholars are quicker to note the presence of what they tend to call rhetorical devices than to comment on their significance, which is the part of the enquiry that interests me. For example, V. Phillips Long in his study *The Reign and Rejection of King Saul*, wrote "the six occurrences of verbal roots containing Rosh and Aleph... may constitute an example of assonantic punning for rhetorical effect (5)." I'm left wondering what that rhetorical effect might be about.

All the same, there are some comments that stood out for me, of which these are my favourites. "The Psalmists used wordplay to entertain, challenge and inspire their readers," wrote Elizabeth Backfish in her study of Psalms ninety to one hundred and five. In Psalm one hundred and one, wordplay "adds poetic beauty to the strophe and poem (6)." Scott Noegel wrote, "The network of Midrashic name derivations, as well as other wordplays, contributes to the high quality of the rhetorical features of the book of Samuel (7)." Stefan Storch considered "The prophets of ancient Israel maximised their use of all the potentialities of their language (8)." Al Walters wrote "Zechariah 4:12 contains a dense system of semantic cross-references and allusions. It is a miniature masterpiece of skilful Hebrew wordplay (9)."

These remarks are more about style of writing than purpose, in my opinion. Perhaps the comment closest to my position comes from Bill Arnold writing about Daniel chapter one, who declares "The narrator's skilful use of wordplay and characterisation tells us exactly who this young man is, and why it is that God used him so mightily in the years to follow (10)." All the same, I find the lack of reflection on the underlying purpose of the literary devices disappointing. To me they are tantalising. What is going on here, I ask myself.

Writing in Hebrew, Moshe Garsiel shows a willingness to note connections between separated stories which I share. He compares Michal lowering David through a window in One Samuel with Michal looking down scornfully at David through a window in Two Samuel. He also compares and contrasts Saul's vow in One Samuel with Jephthath's vow in Judges (11). I did not find other examples of comparison between stories of the kind I find helpful.

I suspect that there might be Midrashic literature that I don't know how to access which may shed light on the approach my enquiry adopts. Take this comment by Rabbi Bahya Ben Asher writing in the thirteenth century for example.

> "The scroll of the Torah is (written) without vowels in order to enable man to interpret it however he wishes... When it is vocalised it has but one single significance; but without vowels man may interpret in it several things, many marvellous and sublime (12)."

Ben Asher's comment implies a measure of lateral thinking about the text which I instinctively find helpful.

The majority of my proposals are to do with subtlety regarding proper names. Here I drew a complete blank with regard to recent studies. My method was to look at the treatment of the story of little Samuel hearing from God at night in commentaries on One Samuel. They filled three shelves in the excellent theological library at Tyndale House, Cambridge. To my astonishment, there are sixty commentaries on the books of Samuel for sale on Amazon currently; I had expected to find just ten or twelve. My wife's guess was closer, at fifteen. Many people have something to say about the book.

None of the books I consulted had noted either of the two links in that story to earlier Israelite leaders arising from their names which I suggest. I seem to be onto something new here. Fun! Or are my ideas so daft that they are not worth considering? You can decide as you read further.

On a different note, my apologies to any readers who feel that as a gentile I have been disrespectful to their scriptures. I researched my family tree over several years to see if I had any Jewish roots and only came up with one Jewish name, that of Bessant, four or five generations back on my mother's side. On my father's side, I have no Jewish connection at all. I therefore have no rights of ownership over the text.

I have enormous respect for the living and enduring word of God. I have attempted to remove the shoes from off my feet and tread delicately on this holy ground. I hope you will feel I have succeeded.

Finally, here's an insight from Richard Bicknell himself which gives the flavour of our enquiry to get us going.

The Hebrew names of the narrative books in the Hebrew Bible tend to comprise the initial word of the text. So Genesis is *Bereshith*, meaning 'In the beginning', and Exodus is *Shemoth* – 'The names', and Leviticus *Wayiqra*, 'And he called out'.

However, the books of Samuel appear to break this rule on first sight by being called simply *Samuel*. But do they?

Have a look at the ninth and tenth words of One Samuel in the Hebrew, reading from right to left. If you run the words 'His Name was Elqanah' together, ignoring the space, you will see the name of Samuel emerge.

שְׁמוֹ אֶלְקָנָה

Elqanah   his   name

שְׁמוֹאֶלְקָנָה

Samuel

I hope the two diagrams make this clear.

Wonderful. Well spotted, Richard.

Samuel's name might have been easier to see in olden times when spaces between words were omitted in manuscripts, presumably to reduce costs. We are so used to the printed word with generous spaces and wide margins on mass-produced paper that it's hard for us to remember how much labour and therefore expense was involved in the production of a book hundreds and even thousands of years ago. Small wonder that early manuscripts do not have spaces between words.

Well, here goes. I hope you find the result stimulating.

What's in a Name?

"Come along, Sickly, don't dawdle. Oh, now where's Wasting gone?"

"He's run off to crisps and sweets again, mum."

Can you imagine this conversation taking place in the aisle of a supermarket between a harassed mother and her toddler? I find I can't. Who in their right mind would call their child Sickly? Or Wasting? But that is exactly what we find at the beginning of the biblical book of Ruth, supermarket excepted that is.

Because there is a famine in Israel, Elimelech, which means 'My God is king', takes his wife Naomi, which means 'Delightful', to live in Moab, along with their two children Mahlon – Sickly and Chilion – Wasting. Why would two parents with such positive affirming names choose names for their children which were frankly demeaning?

Mahlon and Chilion both grow up and marry Moabite women but then die before having children. Their names suggest a connection with their demise. Were they both born without much prospect of a healthy life, and so were named appropriately? Unlikely, it seems to me. Or were their names possibly changed in retrospect to reflect their early deaths?

This is not impossible. Name change in the light of circumstances was not uncommon in those days. Two instances in particular come to mind.

When Jacob's wife Rachel lay dying in childbirth, she called her boy Ben-oni, which means 'Son of my misfortune', but her husband changed the name to Ben-jamin or 'Son of my right hand' (13).

I don't blame Jacob for doing this, to be frank. However, I find it helpful to remember the two aspects of Benoni / Benjamin as I read about his descendants in later times. The tribe is all but wiped out on the road near Rachel's tomb by the brother tribes in the closing chapters of the book of Judges. Benoni indeed. Couldn't the later people have remembered the plea of Jacob to his sons that they were not quarrel with their brother Benjamin on the road (14)?

Later on, King Saul, who was perhaps the most famous Benjaminite, was the Son of God's right hand to begin with, the Lord's anointed, his messiah, but before long it all turned sour and we might say he reverted to Benoni, becoming the son of God's misfortune.

My second example of a name change comes from the second book of Samuel. We read there of Ishbosheth, Son of Saul and therefore the second King of Israel. His name means 'Man of shame'. Really? Can you believe he was called that at birth? I can't.

It seems from the Book of Chronicles that Ishbosheth's original name was Ishbaal, 'Son of Baal' (15). Baal was one of the Canaanite gods that the Israelites were instructed to wipe out. Ishbosheth has to be a deliberate corruption of his birth name, a term of abuse, in my opinion.

There seems to have been a fascination with names, and how the lives of the individuals played out in relation to them. Jacob – 'He grips', was so-named because he was born grasping his twin brother's heel (16). The name also means 'He supplants', and this aspect of his character was seen in the way he cheated Esau out of his birthright and then later the blessing of the firstborn that was due to him (17). Following his conflict with Laban over many years, his name was changed to Israel because he had 'struggled with God' and man and had prevailed (18).

When Jacob's twelve children were born, their names reflected the circumstances of their births.

Reuben, the first born, meant 'See, a son', summing up Leah's delight at giving birth. Simeon came next; his name suggests 'Hearing'. God had heard Leah's complaint. Judah born third turned out to be 'Praiseworthy', as his name implies. There are reasons given for the names of the other nine children in a similar fashion (19).

כלב   כל-לב

Caleb, Dog   heart   all

Other names were not explained but still contained a clue to their owners' character. The name CaLeB sounds like CeLeB – 'Dog'. We are told that Caleb loved the Lord with all his heart; his name can also be thought of as CoL + LeB, meaning 'all heart' or 'whole hearted' (20). As the name, so the man. Both these meanings of his name will turn out to be relevant.

Elijah – 'The Lord is My God', was a man of faith as his name suggests. Indeed, at the climax of the confrontation with the prophets of Baal, when the fire fell from heaven on the drenched sacrifice, the people all called out "The Lord, he is God, the Lord he is God" and in so doing, were as good as chanting Elijah's name (21).

lay waste
sword

Perhaps my favourite instance of a name matching a person's character is SNHRYB or Sennacherib. The Hebrew word HRYB, which comprises the final consonants of his name, means 'to lay waste', with its associated noun HRB meaning 'sword'. King Sennacherib fulfilled his destiny by laying countries waste right and left, but he finally died by the hands of his sons who killed him with the sword, no less (22). Appropriate, we might say.

By now, some readers may be hopping up and down. No, they insist, you cannot do that with names in the Hebrew Bible. Names cannot be manipulated or understood in this way. Take the English word 'greenhouse', for example; there is nothing green about it. It is made of clear glass.

I felt sufficiently chastened when I first heard this argument, but after a few years I realised that while a greenhouse may not appear green itself, its function is to nurture plant life. In so doing, it makes greenery. A greening house, if you like. So rather than the word greenhouse being an argument against seeing meaning in names, it is a call to be rather more subtle in one's appreciation of the hints contained in names, to my mind.

After much pondering of the text, I believe such name play, when noted in the Hebrew Bible, is to be considered and savoured.

גִּדְעוֹן
Gideon

Take Gideon, for example. His name means 'Hacker', from the root GD3. He hacked down his father's altar in the night, then hacked his way through the Midianite army with a band of just three hundred men, and even whacked the Israelites who hindered him in the mopping up operations afterwards (23). I'm not talking about a slavish adherence to some literary principle here; rather, I just note Gideon's hacking and whacking behaviour being true to his name. I am not surprised that he turned out as he did.

I have a similar response to Ehud, who was a left-handed Benjaminite. The idea that a son of my right hand might be left-handed was so unlikely that he was able to smuggle a blade strapped to his right thigh through security without being suspected, and thereby rid the Israelites of Eglon the tyrant who was oppressing them, by driving the blade into his gut with his left hand. Grim but effective (24).

As for the courtiers who failed to protect Eglon, they needed to sharpen up, to be blunt.

I recall a sermon I once heard on the fiery furnace in the book of Daniel (25). This terrible oven, the preacher explained, was made much hotter because of the king's 'bellows'. I have forgotten everything else about that talk except that one play on words. It raised a laugh and held my attention. Maybe the literary devices I am going to propose have a similar function, serving to keep readers involved.

One more thought about a particular Hebrew name. Job's youngest daughter, born after his recovery from his traumatic ordeal, was named Keren Happuch. English translations tend to carry it over in this form. However, in his book *Hebrew Humour and Other Essays*, J Chotzner noted that Keren Happuch means 'Horn (box) of Cosmetics' (26).

That's far more interesting. I immediately have an image of a young person busily applying her black eye-liner. People like to use shortened names with a ring to them; I wonder if she might perhaps have been known by her friends as Zippy, a reference to the fastener of her make-up bag (27)? Always at the height of fashion no doubt.

Let's make the most of the meaning of names in our study.

Samuel and Samson

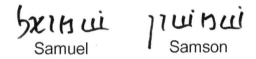

Samuel   Samson

It's time to get to our subject. We will begin with the names of the chief characters.

The first thing we learn on opening the book is that Elkanah's wife Hannah was barren. Hannah prayed, and God intervened. Hannah promised that her boy would be given to God from birth – he would in fact be a Nazirite, abstaining from wine and strong drink and not shaving his head. He would become Israel's judge in due time (28).

All these facts hold good for the birth of the previous judge Samson as well, as we mentioned earlier. Birth following barrenness may not be remarkable, as that had happened to Sarah and Rebekah earlier on, but the giving of the boy that was born to God and especially the Nazirite vow happened uniquely to these two men (29).

There are other features of the Samson and Samuel stories that tend to underline the similarity to

21

my mind. Both are introduced with the same words 'Now there was a certain man from...' In both stories, the focus is on the mother; the father hardly plays any role. In Samson's case, Manoah his dad was not present when the heavenly visitor came to his mother. They prayed that the visitor might come back so that the father could meet him. The prayer was answered, but curiously, the husband wasn't there the second time either. His wife had to run to fetch him.

Similarly, Elkanah, Hannah's husband, shows very little concern for his wife's anguish, and scant interest in her giving up the child to Eli at the temple Shiloh. The importance of what the child would become seems to have passed him by completely.

מָנוֹחַ   מָנוֹת

Manoah   Portions

Finally, here's a strange thing. Samson's dad was MaNOaH – 'Resting place'. Perhaps we can think of him as being laid back. Elkanah gave out MaNOTh at the festival – the commonly used word for portions of a sacrifice that were to be eaten (30). The two words MaNOaH and MaNOTh are similar in Hebrew script. It may be fanciful, but having already noticed the similarities between the births of Samson and

Samuel, my reaction on reading that Elkanah gave out MaNOTh – portions, was to be reminded of Manoah, Samson's father.

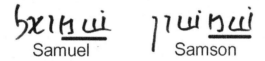

Samuel   Samson

There is of course one more fact to be noted; both names Samson and Samuel begin the same way with the two consonants S and M. Curious.

Samuel and Saul

heard

The meaning of Samuel's name is explained by his mother; he was called Samuel "because I asked the Lord for him (31)." This is to understand the name as SaMu3EL – 'Heard of God', even though the letter Ayin, shown by the number three, is not present in Samuel's name.

Samuel   Saul

There is something strange about this, because over the following verses Hannah repeats a number of times that she 'asked' the Lord for him. The emphasis is more on her asking rather than on her being heard by God.

ask

The Hebrew for ask – ShAL is very like the name Saul. In its intensive form, it can mean 'to dedicate'. Indeed, when Hannah explains to Eli that she is dedicating the boy to the Lord for his entire life, she actually uses the word Saul. Her words are, "He is Sauled to the Lord (32)."

The verbal similarity between the asked-for child and the name Saul does not come over in our English translation. For readers of the Hebrew, the fact that the name Saul should crop up several times when Hannah is talking about Samuel's life and calling may seem a coincidence and nothing more. My reaction, arising from my tendency to notice plays on words, is different. My interest is aroused. To me, it's almost as if Samuel would have been more appropriately named Saul, meaning 'asked for' and even 'dedicated'.

I detect a curious parallelism here. Samuel and Samson have plenty in common, as we have seen, and now it appears that the names of Samuel and Saul also have features in common. What's going on?

S and M, the initial letters of both Samson and Samuel as we noticed before, taken together on their own make up the word for name. This suggests another meaning for Samuel – 'Named by God'. This reminds us of the night-time incident in the temple when Samuel the little boy heard God calling his name, "Samuel, Samuel." Named by God indeed.

Samuel, Saul and David

So Samson, Samuel and Saul seem to be linked. We now come to another curious episode concerning the names of the nation's leaders.

Following his failure to find his father's animals, Saul meets Samuel and discovers more than he bargains for; not only are the asses safe but Saul has been chosen by God to be king of Israel. The spirit of God falls on him to the extent that people ask whether Saul is among the prophets.

After his charismatic experiences, Saul goes to the high place, where he is met by his uncle, who asks him where he has been. Saul explains about his search for the asses, which involved consulting Samuel, but keeps news of the kingship under wraps.

דוד

David / Uncle

Uncle is *DWD* in Hebrew. This is the same word as the name David. David means 'Beloved'. Why an uncle should be any more loved than other family members I don't know. To me the use of DWD to mean uncle feels strange.

Substituting 'David' for 'uncle' in the account of their meeting, as the Hebrew almost invites us to do, we read the following:

> 'Saul's *David* said to him, "tell me what Samuel said"',

and a little later in the conversation,

> 'Saul said, "we came to Samuel." And Saul's *David* said, "what did Samuel say to you?" And Saul said to his *David*...' (33).

I find this curious juxtaposition of the names of the three central characters of the book intriguing. Might it perhaps be an added encouragement to us to note how they relate to each other? These three men are the focus of most of One Samuel, and perhaps a curious quirk of the text underlines that for us.

We barely hear about Saul's uncle again, only that his name was Ner and that he was father of Abner, who would become commander of Saul's army (34). Uncle Ner's appearance is very brief. Indeed, it seems odd to me that he's mentioned at all.

Perhaps it was simply the case that Ner the brother of Saul's father Kish happened to live at the high place where Saul ended up, which is sufficient to explain his presence in the story, and we shouldn't attach any significance to the use of the word DWD. If we take this line, the presence of the word uncle / David need not surprise us.

דוד
David / Uncle / Pot

However, there has after all been an earlier use of the letters *DWD* in the book to mean something other than David. The word also means Pot or Jar or Basket. We read that in the temple, when a sacrifice was being made, the servant of the priest would plunge his three pronged fork into the pan, *DWD* or cauldron and take out whatever the fork brought up (35).

נבל
Nabal / Wine skin

A similar point can be made regarding the word NBL. David will meet Nabal the wealthy farmer later in the book. NBL also happens to mean 'wine-skin', and there is an occurrence of the word when Hannah dedicates Samuel to Eli's care in the temple of the Lord. She takes along a gift of a three year old bull, an Ephah of flour and a NBL of wine (36).

I note that the main thing we are told about Nabal is that he became paralitically drunk in his partying after the harvest. He treated his own body as a wine skin. It seems to have brought on his death. Another example of a name and a destiny being linked.

So the names David and Nabal occur briefly in stories about food and drink at the temple at Shiloh. Is this simply a matter of chance, or is there literary subtlety here? If so, what might that be about?

On reflection, David wanted food from Nabal's harvest, and Nabal refused to give it. Hophni and Phinehas insisted on food from the people who produced sacrifices from the results of their labour, and threatened force if they did not comply. Hophni, Phinehas and Nabal were all close-fisted when it came to food, in an unnecessarily determined manner, and all three paid with their lives.

So are the names David and Nabal as pot and wine skin coincidental to the account, or are they there to encourage us to reflect on possible connections between the two episodes? Hard to say. Let's not attempt to make a judgement at this stage.

Samuel and Joseph

יוֹסֵף יֹסֵף
Joseph add

When I come across the root YSP meaning 'to add' or 'to do again' in the Hebrew Bible, I always ask myself whether it is good to see a possible link with YWSP or Joseph at this point of the story; his name was given when Rachel's hope was that God might 'add' another son (37). Joseph certainly turned out to be a great addition to the family. A crucial one in fact.

The root YSP comes frequently – thirty-three times in the books of Samuel alone. An early instance is found when the Lord calls to Samuel a second and a third time after the lights have gone out in the temple. I read 'and the Lord 'Josephed' to call Samuel', i.e. called Samuel again. In fact the word YSP occurs four times in three verses (38).

Can I gain some insight into the story of young Samuel in the dark by recalling Joseph at this point? I believe I can.

Samuel was in deeper darkness than that caused by the sun going down. The word of the Lord was not often heard in those days, and Eli had allowed his sons to abuse the sacrificial system to the point where their sin was very great in God's eyes, because it brought the Lord's offerings into contempt. Large swathes of Moses' teaching had been given over to careful instructions so that the offerings of the people would be a pleasing aroma to God. Hophni and Phinehas were only interested in what they could get out of it all for themselves. Eli, despite being ninety-eight, severely overweight and blind, did care about the Lord's temple and the ark, but not sufficiently to restrain his sons. They were out of control.

In passing, the two prayers Eli made, for God's blessing on Hannah's prayer for a son and that the Lord would give her more children, were both answered despite his failings. There is hope for us all, even in our darkest moments, it would seem.

Joseph's darkness was also severe. He was rotting in prison, forgotten by the butler and struggling with difficult thoughts about his treatment at the hands of his brothers. Things had seemed so promising in the early days, when he had had those dreams. Where was God now? Not much sense of the word of the Lord being heard.

Well, God had plans to raise Joseph up in order to save the nation, and the same was true for Samuel, from an equally unlikely starting point. Samuel himself saw it that way; he added his own name to the list of deliverers of Israel (39). The Philistines were subdued while he was judge (40). The boy Samuel would himself become a latter day Joseph for the people in time. Interesting.

Samuel and Jephthah

יִפְתָּח
Jephthah

This is how my thoughts ran. Then one afternoon, when I was reading through the story again, I noticed the name Jephthah appearing, when Samuel 'opened' the doors of the house of God in the morning. Jephthah means 'He opens' so we can read it as 'Samuel rose in the morning and 'Jephthahed' the doors of the house of the Lord' (41).

My first reaction was to think, surely there is no connection with the story of Jephthah here. I'm imagining things that aren't there. I need to get a grip.

But then, I reflected that the door of the house which Samuel opened was also a key feature of Jephthah's story in the book of Judges. He had made a vow that on returning from the battle, if he was victorious, he would offer up whatever came out first from the door of his home as a sacrifice.

I then received a shock. There is a strong connection between Jephthah and this story after all. Eli is under condemnation because he honoured his sons more than God even to the point where they were destroying the sacrificial system. They were allowed to run riot; there was no action taken against them at all.

Contrast Jephthah and his crazy vow. I have always thought he should never have allowed such a rash promise to leave his lips, and then I have been even more astonished at the way he carried out his pledge by offering up his only child as a burnt offering to God (42). He honoured the Lord more than his own flesh and blood even to the point of human sacrifice, which had been clearly forbidden. What a contrast with Eli's treatment of his sons.

We even have the use of the word door in both stories, and note also that what is twice referred to as the temple of the Lord and once as the tent of meeting in the early chapters of One Samuel is also called the house of the Lord, as in this instance (43). Jephthah's home, the Lord's home.

Jephthah, his vow and the doors. Hannah kept her promise, made when Eli was sitting by the door of the temple, by sacrificing her only child (at that point) to the Lord. Little Samuel was offered as a living sacrifice. Jephthah also kept his promise to the Lord, but in his case the child's life was forfeit.

Jephthah's daughter came out of the house, and little Samuel came out of the house. Noting the resonances with the earlier story of Jephthah leads to all kinds of insights for me. Thinking about Jephthah because of Samuel 'opening' the doors of the temple has not turned out to be a red herring at all. Fascinating.

Wordplay in Context

At this point, I want to ask a wider question. How might my proposal of word play and manipulation involving names in the Hebrew Bible relate to the culture of the time? Might it be a good fit, or am I trying to impose something without reference to life in that era?

In our own day, we have plenty of evidence to answer such a question. One need go no further than the banner headlines of our national press to see that there is an ongoing use of puns in our society. Hardly a day passes without some form of word play on a name or current event being emblazoned in huge letters on the front of one of our newspapers.

When it comes to the Hebrew Bible, we have little contemporary evidence for the existence of word play in society other than what we find in the text itself, so let's summarise what we observe there.

We begin with the acrostic poems, where each line begins with the next letter of the alphabet. Psalms 25, 34, 37, 111, 112, 119 and 145 contain this feature, and maybe 9 and 10; so do the four chapters of Lamentations and also Proverbs chapter 31.

Actually these thirteen acrostics were not difficult to write, **B**ecause you only need a mildly **C**reative turn of mind in order to **D**o it with **E**ase. Still, the **F**act that the acrostic poems exist in the Hebrew Bible says something about the prevailing culture in my opinion.

There seems to be a possible instance of Gematria in Genesis chapter fourteen. This has to do with the value of Hebrew letters. If you add up the letter counts of Abraham's servant Eliezer (Aleph = 1 plus

Lamed = 30 plus Yod = 10 plus Ayin = 70 plus Zayin = 7 plus Resh = 200) you arrive at 318, which happens to be the number of retainers in Abraham's household, referred to a few verses before Eliezer's name appears (44).

I wonder who discovered that curious fact? Did they also see note that Eliezer means 'God is help', which is exactly what God was for Abraham over the rescue of Lot?

Whether this proposed existence of Gematria is valid or has any significance is less important to us than the fact that it has been unearthed and proposed, which bears witness to an interest in playing with word counts.

הֵ ע בֵ שׁ   לֵ א ו מֵ שׁ
5 70 2 300   30 1 6 40 300
= 377   = 377

We have a possible example of Gematria in our story; the French commentator Rashi - Rabbi Shlomo Yitzchaki or Solomon Isaac, to give him his full name, who lived from 1040 to 1105, reports "some say the *seven* children referred to in Hannah's song have the same numerical count as the name *Samuel* (45)." Seven is SB3H.

Notice that Rashi himself is not impressed by this fact. Personally, I share Rashi's scepticism. Hannah herself had only six children, for one thing (46).

I'm left asking myself how this number parity was discovered. My guess is that somebody added up the letter count for Samuel, found it was 377 and then searched around for other Hebrew words with the same count and was delighted to find the number seven fitted the bill. Hey presto; as SB3H – 'seven' occurs in Hannah's song we have an instance of Gematria.

$$ \text{T} \text{I} \text{T} \quad \text{T'} \text{J} $$

David hand by
4 6 4   4 10
= 14   = 14

Well, two can play at that game. Let's have a go with David – DWD. His name of 4 + 6 + 4 adds up to 14. Can I find a word which adds up to fourteen..? Oh yes, YD 10 + 4, the Hebrew word for 'hand'. Can we find a suitable passage..? Yes, we read that Jesse sent his gift to Saul 'by David's hand', and then just three verses later it was the 'hand of David' on his harp that soothed Saul when the evil spirit from God was on the king (47). An instance of Gematria. Marvellous. Bingo. Jackpot.

You need to ignore the prefix B which means 'by' in the diagram above in your arithmetic. YD DWD, 'hand of David'.

I suppose you might be impressed by my conjuring sleight of *hand* but I'm not. The word YD – 'hand' comes some eleven hundred times in the Hebrew Bible, of which one hundred and eight fall in One Samuel. Seeing a connection between YD and David's name feels meaningless to me.

Allegations of cryptic messages in letters or words or numbers of this kind in the Hebrew Bible are a menace to my mind as they risk cheapening the word of God. You may feel that some if not all of my proposals in this book fall into that category. I have some sympathy with that view, except for the fact that a fair number of the devices I suggest seem to underscore the central issues raised by the text. They are constructive, to my mind, not destructive. This is why they hold my interest.

I invite you to keep an open mind on my proposals until we have finished our enquiry. Let the jury stay out and take time to decide. Then if you conclude I am leading us all up an unhelpful path, please say so and let me know. You will be doing us all a favour. My aim is to be in sympathy with the text, not to undermine it. I want to find hidden riches in it which may have been in the mind of those responsible for it, not impose something tiresome.

Let's move on to another device. In Atbash, the letters of names are swapped with ones at the opposite end of the alphabet. Aleph becomes Tau, Beth becomes Shin etc. The use of the name SSK or Shishak standing for BBL or Babel, i.e. Babylon occurs in two places in Jeremiah, amounting to two instances of Atbash (48). We seem to be on firmer ground here than with the proposed Gematria, but once again, it's the interest in this literary device that is of note.

Incidentally, there was also a king of Egypt in Solomon's day called Shishak in the NIV translation, but in the Hebrew this name ended with a Q. It might be more helpful to translate his name Sishaq in order to distinguish him from the Shishak in Jeremiah (49).

I first came across Atbash 35 years ago and it has taken me all this time to realise how the word is made up – A + T + B + S. Finally grasping what I had never noticed before seems to be the order of the day when it comes to wordplay.

לִפְנֵי   וַיִּפְּלוּ

before   and they fell

There are two pairs of words in the exploit of Jonathan and his armour bearer which have a palindromic feel: WYPLW LPNY – 'and they fell before' Jonathan, referring to the hapless and hopeless Philistine outpost, and T'MTY M'T – 'I tasted a little' honey (50).

מעט טעמתי
a little   I tasted

They are not proper palindromes, and I don't believe they have any literary, theological or spiritual significance as such, but despite this they set my mind working.

My best palindrome in the language of the Hebrew Bible to date is a snappy summary of the book of Jonah.

גדול דג לו
big   fish   to him

It goes LW DG GDWL – 'to him a big fish', or in proper English, 'he had a big fish'. All right, purists might object that the reality was that the big fish had Jonah rather than the other way around, but we will let that pass.

Given the acrostics, Atbash and possible instance of Gematria, one might have thought that palindromes would have an appeal for the biblical authors, but this does not seem to be the case as far as I am aware. I've not come across a single one.

Let's end this section with a quote from Isaiah which makes use of alliteration and assonance, presumably to emphasise a point.

$$\text{ויקו למשפט}$$
$$\text{והנה משפח}$$
$$\text{לצדקה}$$
$$\text{והנה צעקה}$$

This is the conclusion of the story about the disappointing vineyard (51). With no attempt to copy the alliteration, one might translate as follows:

> And he looked for justice
> But behold outpouring
> For righteousness
> But behold a cry.

In the original. 'justice' and 'outpouring' (i.e. bloodshed) are similar, and so are 'righteousness' and 'a cry'. Can you see it? Note that the prefix L in lines one and three means 'for', and the W at the beginning of lines one, two and four usually means 'and' but can mean 'but'.

So here is a rendering that attempts to convey the alliteration even if the concepts have been modified in the process.

> And I wanted a judge,
> but there was only a fudge;
> to be reimbursed,
> but I was only cursed.

I'm glad I am not a Bible translator, and I expect you are too, but at least my clumsy rendering highlights the alliteration.

Riddles

קץ   קיץ

end   summer fruit

Riddles are in evidence in the Hebrew Bible. This conversation between God and the prophet occurs in the book of Amos.

> "What do you see, Amos?"
> "A basket of quince fruit."
> "Yes, and it's quits for my people Israel."

Alright, that's not an exact translation, but it gives the flavour (pun intended), and even manages to preserve the sound of the play on words in the Hebrew, which involves QYtS 'summer fruit' and QtS 'end' (52).

almond tree   watching

On another occasion, Jeremiah saw the branch of an 'almond tree', pronounced ShaQeD, which indicated to him that God was 'watching', pronounced ShoQeD, over his word to fulfil it (53).

Centuries after the text was written, a system of dots known as pointing was added to the consonantal text to give an indication of how the words were to be read, but this was not available originally. Readers had to grasp the meaning and hence the pronunciation from the context. This allows for wordplay and verbal tricks to my mind, as in this instance. Notice that the Lord seems happy to play along. He communicates with us in ways we are used to, understandably.

These two instances from Amos and Jeremiah remind me that riddles were God's normal method of communicating with his prophets. We learn this from the time when Miriam and Aaron opposed Moses in the desert. The relevant passage is worth quoting in full.

> God said, "Listen up. If there's one of your Lord's prophets, I make myself known to him in a vision; I speak to him in a dream. Not so with Moses – he is faithful in all my house. Mouth to mouth I talk to him, by sight and not by riddles, and he sees the Lord in plain view... (54)."

So we are to expect riddles when God communicates through his servants. No wonder we find the writings of the prophets confusing. They strike me as one long puzzle from beginning to end. Indeed, there was so much visual material that Isaiah's writings are summarised as the 'vision' that he received from the Lord; vision is the opening word of the book (55). We refer to the word of the Lord, but did Isaiah receive it all in picture form and have to turn it into poetry and prose himself, I wonder?

One feature of my own dreams is that they are generally strange. Much of the Hebrew Bible reads like a puzzle to my mind. Indeed Ezra and the priests felt the need to make the meaning of even the book of the law crystal clear to the people as they wept over their earlier wrongdoing (56).

Samson set a riddle for the wedding guests arising from his experience with the lion he had killed (57). The story of Samson himself strikes me as a prime example of an enigma; this man was chosen to be a Nazirite, one of God's shock troops as I once heard it explained (58), but he took very little notice of his calling. Indeed, when his story closes and he is described as having judged Israel for forty years, the remark comes as something of a shock. Is being a judge what he thought he was doing? Following in the footsteps of earlier judges such as Ehud, Barak and Gideon? It doesn't feel like it to me.

The Queen of Sheba came to test Solomon with riddles – the same word again (59). She went away impressed. Ecclesiastes and many of the Proverbs of Solomon which aim to untangle the mystery of life contain puzzling passages.

We have two instances of Psalms where the singer declares that he will speak in riddles or parables, numbers forty-nine and seventy-eight (60).

בְּכִנּוֹר בְּנֵי בָּרָ

K B R Q B   K YNB   K R B

There are other passages I could draw on that demonstrate an interest in words for their own sake, such as a phrase in the psalms I enjoy, which when spoken aloud sounds "Bay-rack barn-eye-ik bakir-bake (61)." Delightfully alliterative. It means 'blessing your sons in the midst'.

Can we carry across a feeling of the alliteration into English? 'Sunning your stunning sons' has something to commend it. 'Buoying up your boys' conveys a sense of the wordplay but omits some of the sense. It would be nice to carry over the B, N, K and even the R sounds if possible, but the only English word I can think of in this regard is one that might apply to certain of my proposals in the minds of some readers: 'bonkers'. Never mind.

יֵעָק֗ אֲבָ֫ק יֵזְק֫

יֵזְק֫	אֲבָ֫ק	יֵעָק֗
Jabbok	struggled	Jacob

I also sometimes detect instances of what I call rootplay; for example in the story of Jacob's struggle with his night visitor we find that Jacob at the Jabbok river ABaQ – struggled with his assailant (62). Three similar words, also with an alliterative feel. What might the significance of playing around with words and sounds be in this passage?

All of this adds together. While not everyone will agree with my assessment of the Hebrew Bible as containing word play, it seems to me that there are sufficient grounds for saying that an interest in plays on words and especially in the manipulation of names is not ruled out when we look at the canon as a whole. I'm not proposing an idea which is entirely foreign to the time as hinted at in the text. The idea that there could be subtleties in the stories in One Samuel which invite readers to tease them out is a reasonable one, it seems to me. See if you agree.

Hophni and Phinehas

פנחס   חפני
Phinehas   Hophni

Let's return to the text. It's not always easy to be sure about the value or significance of individual insights; for example, in our own story, the fact that the names of the two sons of Eli Hophni and Phinehas use the same three letters does not strike me as particularly noteworthy, although in the light of our thoughts about the pairing of Samson and Samuel, and then of Samuel and Saul, perhaps it is a little curious (63).

Of more interest is the contrast between our Phinehas, who despised the Lord, and his ancestor Phinehas who was the grandson of Aaron, whose zeal for the Lord was commended. He carried out the death penalty on Zimri the Israelite and Cozbi the Midianite woman Zimri had brought into the camp in breach of the Lord's command. The Lord commended him, and made a lasting covenant of peace with his descendants (64).

This is probably the promise that the Lord revoked when the man of God visited Eli with a message (65). Phinehas Eli's son had presumably been named after his ancestor. We note the contrast between them – the earlier one using a spear with a single point to carry out the Lord's will, and the latter using a three pronged fork to indulge his appetite in a manner that insulted the Lord. It's not hard to see a link between the two Phinehases, but the point is that we don't observe this as the result of any wordplay in the text. The comparison of the two men is more than sufficient on its own.

סְמָחֵ֫נִי

appoint me

However, having said that, I notice that one of the words used by the man of God in delivering God's judgment to Eli is an anagram of the names of Hophni and Phinehas. God's spokesman declares

"He who remains in your house will come and bow down to him (the faithful priest to come, that is) for a payment of silver and a handful of bread and he will say, "*appoint me* to one of your priestly functions so that I can eat (66).""

The word 'appoint me', or 'join me up', is SPHNI, a scrambled version of the names of the two sons of Eli. Curious. I wonder what it might be about.

It occurs to me that one might therefore translate the phrase 'he will say, "put my name down for one of your priestly functions." This would probably have earned me red ink in my school days as being wrong – I was invariably awarded low marks for my translation, but I still like it because the phrase 'put my name down' preserves the notion of the play on the names in an appealing way.

חֲזֵעֲטִי   חֲבֹטֶת   טֹיב''

| despise | see | good |

I note also that the roots B3T – 'despise', BT – 'see' and TYB – 'good', which are used in the man's speech, with their B and T sounds, all come within a few verses; an example of rootplay maybe (67). Any significance? I don't know.

מֵרֵאשִׁית   לְהַבְרִיאֲכֶם

from the beginning   to fatten yourselves

בְּרָא   בְּרֵאשִׁית

he created   in the beginning

These observations are all very well, but I'm more interested in the criticism that Eli and his sons had chosen 'to fatten yourselves from the beginning' (68).

These words remind me of the opening words of Genesis 'In the beginning he created'. Can you see the similarity between these two phrases from the two diagrams (note that the word order is reversed in the second phrase)?

Is there a link between Hophni and Phinehas and the creation story here? Let's consider. God made the world and it was very good. Humanity then spoiled everything through eating the forbidden fruit, and soon afterwards the giving of sacrificial offerings to the Lord by the two sons Cain and Abel went so badly wrong that it led to the death of one of the two brothers.

Now at the temple of Shiloh, Eli and sons had been entrusted with the sacrificial system, God's careful creation as a remedy for sin. It was to have led to a new world of forgiveness and cleansing for the people. The brothers Hophni and Phinehas ruined it all by eating the food used in the offerings in a way that was forbidden, and it led to death once more, this time of both sons in a single day.

Several similarities to chew over.

The Boy Samuel

Let my summarise my thoughts arising from the opening three chapters of One Samuel. The recent history of vows made to the Lord has not gone well; Jephthah's vow resulted in his daughter's untimely death, and Samson's vow meant little if anything to him. In contrast, Hannah's vow and dedication of her boy to Eli's care is going to be a source of good, despite the spiritual darkness of the setting which reminded me of Joseph in prison.

Jephthah's front door had spelt death for his daughter, but when little Samuel opened the doors of God's house on the morning after his vision, I sense that it was a new dawn, almost a new moment of creation. The evening and the morning were the eighth day.

Samuel now knew the Lord, unlike Hophni and Phinehas, whose attitude was contempt for God's creation. Samuel would grow up to be not only a just judge, but also a priest and now that the word of the Lord had started to return, a prophet as well. A latter day Joseph. After much failure, there was a chance to get it right this time. The God of creation was at work.

I could probably have grasped all this simply by reading the Bible in an English translation, but by delving into the Hebrew and noting the points of interest in the text we have been discussing, I have had my senses roused. In particular, the opening of the temple door by the child subject to a vow now has a heightened significance for me. Up to this point I had always passed over it as a minor detail. Noting the plays on words and names has sharpened my perspective, and in my opinion, put me in closer touch with those who wrote the text and their way of thinking.

וְגָדַעְתִּי   גִדְעוֹן

and I will hack off   Gideon

I have a further insight from this passage. God 'declares' – HGD to Eli that as a result of the young men's wickedness, which he knew about but did not stop, God is going to judge Eli's house and GD3 – 'hack' or cut off Eli's descendants (69). GD3 reminds me of Gideon, or Hacker, GD3N who hacked down his father's shrine of false religion and earned the new name of Jerubbaal – He contends with Baal, as a result. Now God is saying that he himself is going to treat Eli's family in the same way. They have turned God's temple into a house of false religion. They and it will be hacked.

Gideon's band of three hundred doggy troops, which I understand to mean whole-hearted troops in the best Calebite tradition (see above), were the means of victory, as Samuel, being faithful in all God's house, would be in his turn for the later generation. There would be victory against the Philistines under Samuel's leadership as there had been against Midian under Gideon.

I have found the wordplays helpful in stimulating thought about the stories. Am I being fanciful, or have I gained a genuine insight into how the minds of the authors worked? Difficult to be sure. Let's continue our study and see where it leads.

We should note in passing that this rejection of Phinehas and his descendants, in stark contrast with the promise made to the earlier Phinehas, is the first of several examples in One Samuel when the Lord appears to go back on his word. We will have more to say about this later.

Ichabod

𝪇𝪇'𝪇

Ichabod

With her dying gasp, Phinehas' wife names her newborn baby AY-KBD – Ichabod, which is generally taken to mean 'No glory', saying in her explanation, "The glory has departed from Israel (70)."

KBD, the second half of Ichabod's name, conveys the idea of weight, whether in a literal sense or a metaphorical one, hence the idea of glory. Some people, on entering a crowded room, immediately gain our attention by their presence; they have KBD.

KBD meaning weight and glory has been used before in our passage. Eli was asked by God, "why did you give your sons more weight than me (71)?" Then just before the account of the birth, we have the comment that the ninety-eight year old Eli was 'heavy' – KBD. This fact contributed to his death.

Personally I prefer the translation of Ichabod 'Where is the glory?' The particle AI can carry the sense of 'where'. I also note that the word used for 'departed' is GLH; this will be used later of Israel going into exile. So a reasonable translation of the verse introducing Ichabod's name might run, Where is the glory, which has gone into exile from Israel (72)?

The word KBD crops up several more times over the following pages. God's hand was *heavy* on Ashdod when the captured ark was put alongside Dagon in their temple (73). There was a very *heavy* tumult of death in the city as a result. When the five leaders of the Philistines finally consulted the priests on how to return the ark to its place, they said it should not go back without a gift – the God of Israel was to be given *weight* (74). Think of what happened to Pharaoh and the Egyptians, they added. Why *harden* your hearts (75)?

The ark would return to Israel in due course, via Beth Shemesh and Kiriath Jearim indicating that God's absence from the nation was only partial and temporary, but years later the glory of God would go into exile once again in the days of Ezekiel. The ark itself was long gone by then. Ezekiel's arresting vision of the heavenly being on his mysterious chariot occurs firstly at the beginning of the book which bears his name; this is the new manifestation of the glory, which is subsequently seen to be departing from Jerusalem and going towards the East, presumably to join the exiles in Babylon, before it finally returns to the brand new temple in Jerusalem at the end of the book (76).

This is perhaps a helpful reminder that although we tend to think of the books of Joshua, Judges, Samuel and Kings as history books, they have traditionally been called the former prophets. So far we have noted links between our stories and Israel's past, particularly that of recent judges. The departure of the ark from the temple is a hint of the promised exile to come, should Israel disobey. Perhaps we would do well to allow Israel's later history to come to mind in our study in addition to seeing continuity with former times, although in my experience, this happens only rarely.

Before we leave the boy Samuel, let's briefly highlight two important remarks. The first is God's saying 'Those who honour me, them will I honour' (77). As the word used here is KBD, we might translate 'Those who give me weight I will give weight to in return'. This principle will be seen at work in Saul's life; he denied God the weight that was owing, and became lightweight himself.

The second noteworthy comment is that Samuel was recognised as being a prophet from early on; not a word of his fell to the ground, or as I prefer to think of it with my interest in humanity's future in space, not a word of his fell back to earth (78). His words all made it into orbit. The word of God had returned with a vengeance. The age of prophecy had begun.

He was somebody who honoured God.

The Ark in Exile

From the moment they capture the ark, there is no peace for the Philistines. Its presence sparks off a plague of rats yielding an outbreak of deadly tumours or haemorrhoids on the bewildered people (79).

עליהם	עלה	לא	עלות	עגלה
upon them	yoke	no	nursing calves	cart

There seems to be some rootplay when the Philistine leaders receive the advice of the priests about how to return the ark to its place. Take a new 'cart' and hitch to it two 'nursing calves' that have 'never been yoked' (80). Note the four uses of Ayin and the five uses of Lamed, L, in just five words.

This alliteration draws my attention to the cart that introduces the phrase. Why the focus on these sounds? Might this word 'cart' – 3GLH remind me of anybody?

עֶגְלוֹן
Eglon

Eglon – 3GLWN springs to mind (81). He was king of Moab, one of Israel's oppressors; we met him earlier when considering Ehud the left-handed Benjaminite. Has he any connection to our story?

At first glance, one would say no. He was an enemy tyrant after all, rather than an Israelite judge. But then, by bringing God's house into disrepute and scandalizing the Israelites who wanted to offer sacrifices there, maybe Eli and his sons had themselves become oppressors of the people, so let's pursue the idea.

הֶעָלִיָּה נְעוּלָה
the upper room   locked

I note first that the killing of Eglon by Ehud is introduced by several words with similar Ayin and Lamed sounds pointing out that it took place in his upper room which was locked (82).

There is a common theme to the two stories, regarding fatness. Eli and sons had fattened themselves on the people's sacrifices (83). The word for fatness recalled the creation story for us. King Eglon was so fat that the blade and haft of the sword

57

were swallowed up when Ehud struck him in the belly (84). In so doing, Ehud killed the fatted 'calf' – 3GLH is very close to 3GLWN, which was normally a feature of good hospitality in those times, but not in this case. The necromancer of En Dor will kill a fatted calf for Saul shortly before his death later in our story, but I digress (85).

Ehud had promised Eglon a secret word from the Lord, which turned out to be the assassination. Eli was likewise given a word through Samuel in a private manner which was a death sentence. The word DBR occurs in both places (86).

There is also an interest in the Jepthahing – opening of the door in both these stories. We discussed Samuel opening the door of God's house and the possible link to Jephthah earlier. We now note that in Eglon's case, the door of the upper chamber played a central role; it was locked shut, and needed to be opened by the embarrassed courtiers before the truth about the sluggish Eglon was known (87). Ehud was nimble on his feet and subsequently led a brisk campaign in which quick thinking and action won the day. At Shiloh, it was Eli who had become sluggish and heavy, and presumably his sons as well. Defeat loomed.

Between them these similarities have got me thinking. The phrase that comes to my mind is from the book of James in what Christians call the New Testament. "You have fattened yourselves in the day of slaughter," James thunders at the abusive employers who did not pay the workers their wages promptly (88). Bad news for ordinary people.

Eli and sons thought they had never had it so good. They had turned the temple into an all-you-can-eat restaurant. It led to their deaths, Eli's from overweight, the boys at the hands of the invading Philistines, and their descendants from having no food because they had no income as priests. The family thought they were doing okay but they had not read the signs of the times rightly. The sword was hanging over them. A bit like Eglon's failure to grasp the significance of the left-handed Benjaminite and his impending blade. He thought he was in charge and had nothing to fear.

הַמְהַמְהֵם	הִתְמַהְמַהּ־אוֹתוֹ
M H M H M Th H	Th W M Th M W H M
hum-humming	mouth-mouthing

There is one more point of vocabulary linking the two stories. When Eglon's courtiers were dithering outside his upper chamber, the word used is

HThMHMHM (89). Let's translate 'While they were hum-humming to themselves', as it preserves the H and M sounds of the Hebrew. While the Philistine leaders and the priests were deliberating in the time of Samuel, the people were making a loud MHWMTh-MWTh sound in their fear (90). In an attempt to preserve the Hebrew sounds, we might say that in their panic they were 'mouth-mouthing off' about their impending death. Hum-humming and mouth-mouthing. Fun.

Incidentally, the courtiers thought that Eglon was covering his feet, i.e relieving himself, when actually he was being killed. This theme will resurface when David encounters Saul relieving himself in the cave. On that occasion, Saul will escape being killed by the narrowest of margins. The plot thickens.

God on the Move

When the Philistines finally decide that the ark is too hot to hold, they return it to Israel. The milk cows pulling the cart stay on the road helpfully, turning neither to the right – YMYN or left – SMAOL (91).

ימין
right

שמאול
left

בִּן־יָמִין   שְׁמוּאֵל
Benjamin   Samuel

These words for right and left in the Hebrew remind me of Benjamin – BN-YMYN and Samuel. The story will soon focus on two men, Saul, from the tribe of Benjamin, and Samuel, the judge *cum* prophet *cum* priest.

The cows keep straight on. The Hebrew word used is YSR, pronounced YaShaR, implying uprightness or integrity. Our phrase 'right down the line' springs to mind.

YaShaR recalls for me the repeated comment in the closing chapters of the book of Judges that 'there was no king in Israel and the people did what was 'right' – YaShaR, in their own eyes' (92).

I note a number of connections involving place names between our story and the final era of the book of Judges. When the six hundred Danites were on the move in that time, looking for a home, they camped close to Kiriath Jearim on their way north before enticing the Levite away from Micah's shrine (93). In our story, on its way back from the Philistines, the ark was looking for a home. It would rest at Kiriath Jearim for twenty years. Hophni and

Phinehas were both drawn away from their shrine too.

Both stories have a theme of superstition; having a Levite on board and having the ark with you were seen as ensuring God's presence, somewhat like a mascot. But this was perverse; in both stories, the house of God is stated as being at Shiloh (94). You can't strong arm the ark of God or his servant into supporting your cause by getting them to do a walkabout at your pleasure.

In the following story in Judges, a different Levite is found taking his concubine back home; he needs to find a stop for the night. He opts for Gibeah in Benjamin (95). In the later time, this will be Saul's home town, remarkably, because following the hideous outrage that took place at Gibeah at the end of the book of Judges, which recalled the events at Sodom long before, all Israel had been summoned by the grisly means of sending round the body parts of the dismembered concubine, and the subsequent war of vengeance resulted in the complete destruction of Gibeah and its people. So how could Gibeah already be flourishing as a town once again in Saul's day, we wonder?

Saul would in his turn send round body parts to summon the troops. This time, they would be pieces of cows rather than of a human, thankfully.

Incidentally, an alternative stopping place for the night considered by the Levite in Judges was Ramah, which also features in One Samuel since it was Samuel's home town (96).

Another link between the closing chapters of Judges and one Samuel is the fact that Jabesh Gilead features in both. In the earlier story, the inhabitants had failed to attend the muster, and so were summarily killed; in the later one, they are overrun by Nahash the Ammonite and subsequently rescued (97). It is because King Saul was so outraged by the attack on the people of Jabesh that he dismembered the pair of oxen and sent their body parts round all Israel to summon the troops, copying the earlier deed in Judges, as we noted earlier (98).

We should perhaps add that the threatened gouging out of the right eyes of the people of Jabesh Gilead recalls the gouging out of Samson's eyes (99). Yet another link. So too the ark returned by the faithful cows arrived at Beth Shemesh, whose name with its double S also reminds me of Samson (100).

In addition, the dancing girls who were seized to provide wives for the remaining Benjaminites in the sorry conclusion of the earlier stories were from Shiloh, which again features strongly in One Samuel (101).

All these points in common between the final chapters of Judges and the accounts in One Samuel comprise added encouragement to me to hold the stories in Judges and One Samuel firmly together. I feel the need to view Judges and One Samuel as a whole. The stories are not isolated events; they comment on each other.

I am intrigued. What is all this interplay between the two times trying to tell me?

Samuel and His Sons

There is more to say about Nahash, but for now, we need to retrace our steps a little. It's easy to pass over what appears to be a throwaway remark but one which I find arresting.

When Samuel becomes old, he appoints his sons as judges, but they turn out to be corrupt. They go in for dishonest gain, accept bribes and pervert justice (102).

There are few things less acceptable in the Hebrew Bible than an unjust judge. The Lord hates false scales, bribes and the rest of it (103). Eli was taken to task severely for not correcting his wayward sons, but what do we find here? Not a hint of criticism of Samuel from God. It seems that Eli can do nothing right, and Samuel can do nothing wrong. How can this be?

Eli's sin brought the sacrificial system into disgrace and even ruin. Samuel's failure to correct his boys brought down the judicial system. The elders of the people tell Samuel they would rather have a king instead. No more judges for the nation, thank you.

When Samuel prays about their request, he receives understanding and sympathy from the Lord. The people are to be allowed a king despite all the problems the new state of affairs will bring. The rejection Samuel is experiencing is the same rejection that God feels.

I find it bewildering not only that Samuel receives no censure but also that we only hear briefly about his appalling sons because their conduct explains the people's desire for a king. It's as if God does not care about the sons' behaviour. How can he be so down on Eli but so lenient on Samuel? Where is the steadfastness of God, who would say to Malachi later, "I the Lord do not change (104)?"

I find this inconsistency baffling.

Saul on the Move

Following the request for a king, we now get to meet Saul. His father sends him and a young man off to look for asses that have strayed. Their wanderings lead them finally to a town in Zuph, presumably Ramah, where Samuel the prophet lives. Saul and the young man have the idea of asking Samuel for guidance.

Saul seems to need a lot of prompting in his life. The need for guidance will one day drive Saul into a nocturnal séance, but that's for later on.

יֹוסֵף   יֹסֵף
Joseph   Add

The two young men are nervous about meeting the great man. They decide to take a gift of silver with them. The wording of the text is worth noting. It involves the word YSP – add, which resembles the name of Joseph, as we saw before. We read 'And the young man 'Josephed' to answer Saul and he said... (105)'. Biblical Hebrew in prose passages can be verbose at times, so this turn of phrase is not perhaps as clumsy a way of talking as it might sound to us, but all the same, the mention of our friend Joseph once again feels somewhat redundant and therefore makes me pause.

66

Saul and his young man have run out of food, and feel the need for help. Their nervousness at approaching the man of God, their concern over an appropriate gift, the mention of silver and Samuel's greatness as leader of the people all relate to the story of Joseph the ruler of all Egypt and the visit of the ten anxious brothers presenting their silver to buy food (106).

In their case, the brothers got far more than they bargained for; not only was there food and to spare for them and their households, with an especially large portion for Benjamin at the meal at noon; the brothers were themselves treated like royalty and ended up living in Goshen, the best part of the country.

In our story, on meeting Samuel, there is also an abundance of fine food for Saul the Benjaminite at the midday meal (roast leg, presumably of lamb, yum yum), and Saul is going to have his life and prospects changed unexpectedly. Royalty beckons. It must have been a dizzying experience for Saul as it had been for the brothers and later their father in Joseph's presence.

We noted earlier that little Samuel and young Joseph would both be elevated to become saviours of the people. Samuel has since matured into this role. Now Saul turns up, and we find ourselves thinking of Joseph once again. This prompts the question, will young Saul tread a similar path and become the saviour of the nation?

At this point, the dreams of the butler and the baker who were in the prison with Joseph seem relevant too. Both dreams were about being raised up out of prison – the butler to high office and the baker to hanging on a high branch of a tree (107). An intriguing resemblance to Samuel flourishing on the one hand and Saul coming to grief on the other.

Looking to rise up in life? To get to the top? Be careful what you wish for. I'm told that in feudal England, there used to be two classes of people, the eorl and the ceorl. Over time, one proved to be upwardly mobile and became an earl; the other did less well and became a churl. Samuel and Saul all over again, one might say.

You see? I did sometimes listen at school.

I find the web of interconnections between different parts of Israel's experience fascinating and intriguing. All that came from observing the use of the root YSP. Remarkable.

$$\text{נ}\text{ב}\text{י}\text{א} \quad \text{,מה}$$

bring   we   what

I note a further point of interest in the story. When considering the gift to take to the man of God, Saul asks the young man, MaH NaBY – 'what shall we bring' (108). MaH means 'what', the prefix N conveys the pronoun 'we', and BY is from the word 'to come', so the sense is, 'what shall we cause to come', i.e. what shall we bring.

$$ \text{X·IJ} \quad \text{.7b} $$
prophet   what

In using this verbal form, Saul happens to use the word for prophet – NaBY. Taken out of context, we would understand MaH NaBY to mean 'what is a prophet' but in this context it should be translated 'what shall we bring'. The phrase taken on its own has two meanings (109).

Samuel is the archetypical prophet by this point. Not only do all his words rise up into orbit, as we saw before, but everything he predicts about Saul's coming day comes true. The moment Samuel has anointed Saul with oil, he immediately starts announcing to Saul the schedule of his wanderings for the day, including what others will say and do when he meets them. Not only so, but Saul himself is going to get drawn into prophecy as a result of his experiences.

Prophecy is the theme of the hour. Samuel's skill at prediction is extraordinary. Man can hear from God. But is foretelling really the heart and soul of prophecy? Samuel's idea of kingship seems to have been that the leader should hear from God and rule accordingly. (What a good idea for those in charge of synagogues and churches and nations. Don't get me started...). How will it actually turn out, we wonder? Will Saul pick up this particular baton? Is Saul also among the prophets?

The Request for a King

In asking for a king, the people are Sauling for a king – Saul means 'asked' as we noted earlier. The word comes several times (110). Samuel, we remember, has the same four letters as Saul but with an additional M in the middle. His name means 'Heard of God' you recall. The interplay between the two men will dominate the next few chapters of the book.

We learn that Saul is small in his own eyes, and from the most insignificant clan of the tiniest tribe, but that physically he is head and shoulders above the people. This latter fact is mentioned twice, which alerts us (111). Any significance here?

Goliath of Gath, who would challenge the Israelites to provide an opponent in single combat, was six cubits and a span, which amounts to a similar height (112). Saul and Goliath looked each other in the eye, above the heads of everyone else. The implication is that Saul should have taken him on, not young David.

There may be a hint of that in the text. It was while David was talking to his brothers that Goliath strode forward to challenge Israel. The text says Goliath came out and stood 'between the two of them'. This is rather strange in context. Presumably it means between the two armies, but the syntax would have earned red ink from my teachers at school.

בֵּנְיָמִין   בֵּנַיִם

Benjamin   between the two
of them

It so happens that the Hebrew word pronounced BeNaYM – 'between the two of them' comprises most of the name Benjamin – BeNYaMYN (113). Note that M changes shape slightly when it is the final letter of a word. Maybe it's a subtle hint that Saul the Benjaminite should have stepped forward in single combat. Intriguing.

שׁ ג ם
shoulder / Shechem

There may also be significance in the twin use of the word 'shoulder'. In Hebrew, it is SCM, Shechem. The city of Shechem was named from a shoulder of land, true, but I find myself thinking of Shechem the Canaanite, who raped Dinah the daughter of Jacob and then claimed he had fallen in love with her. The story comes from many years earlier (114). Levi and Simeon appeared to support Shechem's suit to begin with, but acted treacherously; while the Shechemites were still in pain from undergoing circumcision as part of the deal, the two brothers killed them all.

Saul seemed to be a good find for the nation to begin with, but he turned out to be treacherous too. Is the reference to his shoulder when we first meet Saul significant, or is it no more than a chance similarity to the earlier man Shechem? Hard to tell.

The word shoulder comes a third time. We read that it was as Saul turned his shoulder away from Samuel that God changed his heart (115). To begin with, it was the spirit of God that fell on Saul from time to time, but after a while, an evil spirit from God will be falling on him as his jealousy of David takes an increasingly firm hold. He will even try to kill his son Jonathan with a javelin when the mood is on him. He

72

is not the only leader to have looked promising to begin with but turned out to be treacherous when in office. Interesting. It helps me feel that the connection with the earlier Shechem should be kept in mind.

Nahash

נָחָשׁ

Nahash / serpent

We have now caught up with NaHaSh once again, the Ammonite king who challenges the people of Jabesh Gilead (116).

His name means 'snake' or 'serpent', recalling the scene in the garden of Eden. That creature was described as being the most 'subtle' of the beasts of the field; at least, we think that is what it means, but as the word 3RWM has been used in the preceding verse to describe the man and his wife as being 'naked', its precise meaning is somewhat elusive (117). Jealous Saul will lie down 'naked' all night in his failed attempt to seize David later on; he and his bands of men all end up prophesying (118).

Let's go with the traditional translation 'subtle' here. What strikes me about our Nahash is how incredibly unsubtle he was. He threatens the people with having their right eyes gouged out. They say, okay, but give us a week first to try to get help, and if that fails we will agree terms. Nahash nods his head and stands back in a gentlemanly fashion so that the diplomacy can take place. Saul hears about it, dismembers the cows, the nation turns out, and Nahash and his people are obliterated. How barmy is that?

The serpent in the garden promises Adam and Eve that if they eat the forbidden fruit, which was good to look at, their eyes will be opened. The snake that Moses put on a pole in the desert was a source of healing for the people, if they looked at it (119). By the time of King Hezekiah, long after our story, that snake had become an object of worship; it was being looked at in the wrong way, so Hezekiah destroyed it (120). In our story, Nahash wants to gouge out right eyes. Four snake episodes all to do with eyes and seeing. Interesting.

We found ourselves remembering the creation from a proposed rootplay to do with Eli's sons. Now we are reminded of the dawn of time once again. Intriguing. Let's hold this in mind and see where it leads.

Hebrews Crossing Over

עבר
cross over

The root *3BR*, which means to pass or cross over in its verbal form, and 'beyond' when used as a preposition, comes an unusually large number of times in a few verses in the next story to my mind. I am hesitant to read too much into this, as the root is a very common one, but nevertheless, the repetitions here caught my attention.

The story is about Jonathan and his armour bearer 'crossing over' the 'pass' between 'crossing points' to attack the Philistine outpost. The verbal root 3BR comes seven times in eight verses (121).

עברים
Hebrews

While this is going on, the nation normally called Israel has been referred to as 'Hebrews' three times in the previous chapter. "Oh look, the Hebrews are coming out of their caves," the Philistines scoff when Jonathan and his armour bearer reveal themselves (122).

Hebrews are 3BRYM, ones that cross over, also using the root 3BR. The word comes five times referring to the nation (123), and on a sixth occasion the five consonants are again used to mean ones that cross over (124).

So what's all this emphasis about crossing over and Hebrews? This verbal repetition highlights for me the fact that some of the Hebrews crossed the Jordan to get away from possible conflict (125). One moment, I say to myself; this eastward movement across the Jordan was to undo the earlier westward movement of the invasion and conquest. Some people of the nation that crossed over from Egypt to the promised land in victory are now making the journey in reverse in defeat. How grim is that. This theme of retreat beyond the Jordan will resurface at the battle of Aphek on Mount Gilboa at the end of the book.

The instruction had always been that the people were not to fear the warrior inhabitants of the land, as the Lord would give them victory. Now things are very different. The Israelites have given way to fear.

Note the contrast with Jonathan and his armour bearer, who 'cross over' towards the Philistines, using hands and feet in a stiff upward climb, and achieve a significant victory against all the odds.

When the outcome of the battle becomes clear, the ones who had hidden across the Jordan and in caves and pits rejoin their comrades. But Jonathan has demonstrated that the Lord gives victory by many or by few, as he puts it (126).

יְהוֹשֻׁעַ   וַיֹּשַׁע

Joshua   and he saved

God had saved the people – the word for 'saved' uses the name Joshua which serves to underline the point about crossing the Jordan to my mind (127).

Saul's Fear Proves his Undoing

Before and after Jonathan's victorious exploit, we are given two reasons as to why Saul lost the kingship.

On the first, his army started drifting away until it was reduced to six hundred men, and when Samuel failed to arrive after the promised seven days, Saul went ahead in fear and offered the sacrifice to gain God's favour.

Samuel arrived moments afterwards, and told Saul that by so doing he has broken God's instruction; this will cost him the kingship (128).

On the second occasion, Saul did not carry out the Lord's instruction to the letter either; he preserved some of the booty of the defeated Amalekites in defiance of the Lord's ban out of fear of the people. It falls to Samuel once again to deliver the Lord's judgement (129).

Both times, Saul made out that he had done nothing wrong and protested his innocence. Note the contrast with David, who in due time would fail over the matter of Uriah and Bathsheba. When his sin was pointed out to him, he immediately made a full and unreserved confession, unlike Saul (130). David did not lose the kingship for his misdeed, as Saul would do, but he did see war in his own family for the rest of his days as a result of his actions.

So this time is characterised by fear in the nation, with nobody more fearful than the king himself. Not a good state of affairs.

מוֹרָא   מוֹרָה

fear   razor

It's worth mentioning a suggestion of Rabbi Jonathan at this point. He translated Hannah's promise to God about her child Samuel 'no razor will come on his head' as 'no fear of man will come on him', in line with a possible reading of MWRH as

MWRA (131). We note that people were afraid of Samuel – Saul on his initial approach when searching for the asses, and Jesse and the elders of Bethlehem when Samuel arrived in town unexpectedly (132). Samuel was confident in all his dealings. He does not seem to have been afraid of anyone.

Personally, I am not convinced by this suggestion as a translation. MWRA only comes this once in the Hebrew Bible, and we infer that it means 'fear' or 'terror' from the context. The same applies to MWRH to mean 'razor' from these two uses to describe Samson and Samuel. It too comes nowhere else.

I prefer the thought that the word 'razor' being similar to 'fear' might suggest to readers that as well as not shaving their heads, the two men would be fearless in life. Even more than Samuel, Samson seems to have had no fear at all. All the stories about him witness to his complete lack of caution, it seems to me. He was brave and foolhardy to the Nth degree.

I see a possible significance in the number of Saul's army being six hundred (133). It may not sound very many compared to the Philistines who were as the sand of the seashore, but Gideon had started out with an army of thousands and had it reduced by the Lord to a mere three hundred, which was half as many as Saul's six hundred. Gideon's men were troops that drank like a dog, or as I understand it, were Caleb-like i.e. stout hearted, as we discussed earlier (134).

Saul's six hundred men would prove to be just as faithful – there were still six hundred of them a while later when Saul was sitting under his pomegranate tree (135). They did not need their resolve to be stiffened by the offering of the sacrifice.

וַאֶת אָפֵק

Apheq

In Saul's attempt to justify his action, he said 'and I forced myself' to make the offering (136). The root of this word is APQ, and I note that the Philistines would gather at APheQ before the final battle in which Saul's life would come to an end, as they had also done in the time of Eli (137). It's as if at the very moment of his fall from grace, Saul's death at the hands of the Philistines was forecast. This reminds me once again of the garden of Eden, where the serpent promised Adam and Eve that if they took the fruit, they would not surely die (138). This was false; the moment they ate the fruit they brought themselves and the human race under the pall of death even though the carrying out of the sentence was delayed.

מעדנת

Eden

I find this thought about Apheq confirmed by a word used about king Agag on the second occasion of Saul's fall. He had been spared from the death penalty carried out on the Amalekites, in breach of God's command. When summoned, he thought to himself, surely the bitterness of death is passed. He walked over M3DNT. Some translate this as 'in chains' or 'bound', but this is to presume that the root was originally 3ND and has somehow become scrambled into 3DN (139). This proposal seems unsatisfactory.

Incidentally, I do apologise for all these uses of 3 to stand for the letter Ayin. It's too bad that we don't have Ayin in our English alphabet. Perhaps changes could be made to our language, so that it could be incorporated? It would simplify things.

Back to the text. Personally, I note that 3DN means Eden, and so I think to myself that Agag 'Edened' his way over to Samuel. The root means 'luxury', 'dainty' or 'delight'; that garden enjoyed briefly by Adam and Eve must have been a wonderful place (140). With his relaxed mindset, I imagine Agag adopted a cheeky shuffle or maybe a jaunty walk. Or were the four seasons in place at the dawn of time?

If so, we might say that Agag walked over with a Spring in his step. Saul has been soft; surely Samuel the old man will be soft as well. Best to strike a light note.

As it turned out in the garden of Eden for Adam and Eve, this confidence that Agag has got away with it will be short lived. Their death took a while to come about; Agag is hacked in pieces before the Lord promptly.

The Rise of David

Saul's downfall has come about for two reasons. In a similar manner, David's rise seems to have had two causes. Firstly, he was a good harpist and was able to calm Saul when the evil spirit from God was on him, and secondly he was a fearless young shepherd whose experience with lions and bears enabled him to slay Goliath.

אַדְמוֹנִי

reddish

One word appears in both accounts. David is described as ADMWNY when he enters Samuel's presence during the search for the next king among Jesse's sons, and Goliath, when looking over the young David in contempt, uses the same word to describe him (141). The traditional rendering of this word is 'ruddy', arising from the root ADM meaning 'of a reddish complexion', a characteristic David shared with Esau who was consequently referred to as Edom. Perhaps the colour referred to was an earthy one – ADMaH with an H at the end means 'earth'.

I prefer to think of David as being Adamic. Let's consider the connection between David and Adam, which takes us back to the garden of Eden yet again. God's aim then had been to create the perfect humanity in his own image. The project went sadly wrong. By the time of Samuel, I see God's repeated attempts to get humanity back on the right path despite human weakness. The priesthood has tanked? Never mind, let's move onto the prophets. The judges have fizzled out? Let's try a king; not God's idea, not even a good idea, but it could succeed given a leader who followed the Lord with all his heart.

Oh dear, the first king did not work out. But maybe David will turn out to provide this Adamic reset. Dare we hope for something better this time than Eli with his lax ways, Samuel's sons being unjust judges, and Saul fearing the people more than the Lord?

I love the way the Lord never gives up on us. We may be seated in the ash heap, but he reaches down to lift us up, to quote the Psalmist. Don't we need that in our day. What a mess we are in.

Goliath of Gath

נת   גלית
Gath   Goliath

The name Goliath of Gath has a pleasing ring to it. I have been trying to think up a modern equivalent. Anne of Athelhampton, Roger of Rotherham, Bill of Bristol, Suzy of Sudbury, Lyn of Lymington and perhaps my favourite Oscar Kokoschka of Austria the artist – I don't find any of them as good as Goliath of Gath.

We are told that Goliath was from Gath twice in this passage. Later on, when David accepts the sword of Goliath from Abiathar he immediately goes to King Achish at Gath (142). I wonder therefore whether the author of the book enjoyed the alliteration.

גלית
Goliath

In addition, the LY in the middle of Goliath's name, the part of it which differentiates it from Gath, means 'to me', and I note that during the verbal sparring before their fight, Goliath invites David to come LY – 'to me' (143).

bronze   Nahash

Goliath's equipment is made of bronze – the word NHoSheTh comes four times in quick succession (144). It is the name Nahash with an extra T on the end, recalling the serpent of Eden once again. Goliath uses fear as his main means of attack. Snaky.

I also note that God gave Eden to Adam as a home for birds and animals for him to name. They would be in fear of humanity. Now the tables are reversed; Goliath promises that rather than man ruling over them, the birds and animals have become objects of fear as they will feed on the man's flesh (145).

Saul should have taken Goliath on, as we noted earlier; the two are of similar height. It therefore feels a bit rich for Saul to give David equipment and instructions as to how to go about the fight, as if he is some kind of expert in mortal combat.

I enjoy David's response to Saul; "Don't let the heart of Adam fall (146)." Adam means 'man', another reference to Eden.

Doeg the Edomite

דֹאֵג
Doeg

The story moves on. Saul allows his jealousy of David to take a grip to the point of wanting to kill him and David finds himself on the run from Saul. He asks Ahimelech the priest to help him with food and a weapon, which he does despite his reservations. This is witnessed by Doeg the Edomite, Saul's head shepherd.

When Saul discovers from Doeg that Ahimelech has let David get away, he is furious. Ahimelech protests his ignorance, but that is no good. Doeg is ordered to kill him and the other priests of the Lord, eighty-four in total. He does not stop there, killing all the inhabitants of Nob, including wives, children and infants, and the cattle, donkeys and sheep as well (147).

How dreadful. Ahimelech means 'My brother is king', but now that Saul is on the throne, any sense of brotherly feeling for this Israelite has evaporated.

Note too the level of savagery. I have a friend who cannot cope with the god of the Old Testament, as he puts it, because of his command to kill off whole races. He sees God as guilty of genocide.

I don't have an answer that satisfies him, but I do note from a number of our stories that vengeance was ruthless in those days. All the inhabitants of Shechem were killed by Levi and Simeon, not just Shechem himself. Nahash wanted to make all the inhabitants of Jabesh Gilead blind in one eye. David's reaction to Nabal's insult will be to want to kill every male in his household, and he will think nothing of polishing off whole villages when he and his men are based at Ziklag (148). From all this, I have the impression that warring tribal factions in continuous conflict to the death was a feature of those times. We do well therefore to see God's instructions that cause my friend difficulty in the context of the age, it seems to me.

Returning to Saul, what a long way he has come. His first encounter with Samuel the man of God had been a nervous one – would the paltry sum they had to offer be enough? Now his ruthless action towards the priests of the Lord bears all the hallmarks of the worst of the world's tyrannical regimes. Horrible.

רֹאֶה   רֹעֶה   רֹעִים

seer   shepherd   shepherds

There may be a hint of what is to come in Saul's original encounter with Samuel. There we are told that Samuel was a RoEH, a seer (149). Doeg, we discover, is the Ro3eH or shepherd of Saul's livestock (150). The word comes in its plural form.

The two words 'seer' and 'shepherd' are spelt differently, but they have a similar sound. While we don't know for sure, the letter Aleph in the middle of seer seems to have carried very little weight, somewhat like the smooth breathing in ancient Greek. Ayin, the middle letter of shepherd which I represent by 3, is more like Greek's rough breathing. The grammar from which I learned Hebrew says of Ayin that it "is very difficult to pronounce, being produced at the back of the throat, almost like a gulping sound (151)." This particular skill continues to elude me – perhaps you would like to try it, with a glass of water standing by in case of emergency. While my experience of hearing Hebrew spoken may not be representative, to my ear most speakers would not differentiate much between the sound of the two words 'seer' and 'shepherd' in practice.

דאג
Doeg / worry

This similarity between 'seer' and 'shepherd' may not amount to much on its own, but it so happens that Doeg's name also came up in the earlier story. In discussion with his young man, Saul wonders whether they should return home as his father will stop thinking about the donkeys and start 'worrying' or 'Doeging' about the two of them (152).

As with all these other proposed plays on names in the text, this may be a coincidence, but nevertheless the occurrence of Doeg's name in advance causes me to reflect. Suppose Saul and his companion had gone home, and never met Samuel the RoEH, and Saul had not been anointed king, what then? The savage brutality of Doeg the Ro3eH would not have entered his life. Perhaps we could have gone straight to David the Ro3eH instead.

As it is, we are told that there was no one better in Israel than Saul, and that God had chosen him to be his anointed king. Everything looked rosy; Saul was the messiah being initiated into prophecy within hours of meeting Israel's leader Samuel. So exciting. But we now see a small shadow during that original encounter, the name of Doeg coming into the story as a tiny warning of horrors to come.

This is in a similar vein to the insight we had about Saul and Aphek earlier. The hope was that Saul would become a prophet, like Samuel. Do I detect a hint of a prophecy in these possible wordplays of Saul going over to the dark side? The end of the story is going to be grim. Saul, already troubled by an evil spirit from

God, will end up consulting a medium when he no longer hears God's voice, and coming to grief soon afterwards. Fascinating.

Saul and Samuel – a Reprise

As you can probably tell, I am feeling my way through the text as I go. Now that we have had further thoughts linking back to Saul's arrival in the story, let's retrace our steps and summarise what is going on in the earlier passage. It will help me even if it doesn't help you.

The fine young man who went off to look for his father's missing asses – none better in the whole of Israel – was head and Shechem above his fellows. (Hint of treachery to come?) He and his young companion passed through the region (Hebrewfied the region? The root 3BR comes four times in one verse) and then became concerned that Saul's father would start Doeging – worrying about them.

"Let's visit the local man of God," declares his assistant, "perhaps he will tell us our fortune."

"Ah," replies Saul, "but what shall we bring (= what is a prophet) the man, as our food is gone and we have no silver (recalling the brothers' approach to Joseph)." In his reply, the companion added (Josephed) that he had a little silver which would do.

Incidentally, the man of God of those days was known as a RoEH (seer, compare Doeg the Ro3eH – shepherd).

"Let's do it," declares Saul.

When they get to the town, they meet a gaggle of girls on their way to draw water, not unlike Moses meeting Jethro's daughters at the well in Midian (153). The girls instantly supply the local gossip at considerable and perhaps unnecessary length. As Rashi observed, "They prolonged their conversation in order to gaze on Saul's handsomeness" (154).

God has spoken to Samuel the day before about the Benjaminite who is coming to save (Joshua) the people from the Philistines "because I have seen my people and their cry has come to me (similar to God's words to Moses at the burning bush)." Samuel and Saul meet in the gateway (all important business in ancient times took place at the city gate) and Saul says "you're to eat with me today, and I will sort you out in the morning. Don't worry about the asses – now found – it's you that Israel wants."

The biggest portion of food is served to the Benjaminite Saul (recalling Joseph serving the brothers lunch and giving Benjamin the lion's share) and next morning, he is anointed with oil for his new role. Samuel encourages Saul to discover the world of prophecy by a day of initiation, leaving people asking the question Is Saul also among the prophets?

I have proposed a considerable number of plays on words and literary subtlety. You may find them interesting, or you may not.

To me, the passage opens up two possibilities for us. Is Saul, the first king of Israel, going to follow in the footsteps of former great leaders of the nation, like Joseph, Moses, and Joshua that seem to me to be hinted at? Or will he turn out to be treacherous like Simeon and Levi slaughtering the inhabitants of Shechem and Doeg annihilating the priests and their families?

I propose that the literary devices I have alleged serve to underscore this key issue of the text.

I find the role of the supernatural fascinating here. Samuel is hoping that Saul will embrace a life of prophecy. Well things look promising to begin with, but in the end Saul is going to follow a path into the occult. Consulting the medium of Endor will prove to be his final undoing.

Perhaps there is a hint of how things are going to go in this regard even at this early stage. When Saul and his companion discuss approaching the man of God, the scene does rather remind me of someone wondering about seeking out the gypsy with a crystal ball in a tent in a fairground, which was a familiar scene in my youth. I suppose the modern equivalent would be attending a Body, Mind and Spirit gathering and seeking a consultation. I get the impression that despite his fine sounding words and actions, for example in the matter of offering a sacrifice to God to win God's support for the coming conflict, maybe Saul's relationship to God had a considerable component of superstition in it and was more apparent than real.

It all looked so promising, but it was going to go horribly wrong. So sad.

David and Saul in the Cave

Alert readers will have noticed that my proposed literary devices are not evenly spread through the text. I don't know why they should be. Perhaps I'm missing some instances.

The next point of interest that seizes my attention comes further on in the story. David is on the run in earnest, and there comes a point when he and his men are hiding in a cave, and Saul comes in to relieve himself – to cover or overshadow his feet as the Hebrew puts it, presumably to imply his long robe being spread out round him as he squatted (155).

Saul has brought along three thousand men with him. This is the same number as the men of Judah that came earlier to deal with Samson at Lehi. On that occasion, after his victory, Samson nearly died of thirst; God opened the rock for him and water gushed out, as had happened with Moses in the desert at an earlier time (156).

Samson had holed up in a cave much as David has done in our story. Are we therefore to consider David in the light of Samson in these chapters?

There has already been a hint of this. Saul's earlier behaviour towards David has been like that of Samson's enemies. The father of the Timnite girl that Samson had tried to marry gave her to Samson's friend instead. "Have her younger sister", he urged. Saul did something similar to David with his two daughters Merab and Michal (157). Then again, Saul sent David out to fight in the hope was that he would fall by the hand of the Philistines. This recalls the words of Delilah, "The Philistines are upon you Samson." She was recruited by the Philistines to get Samson once and for all (158). Finally, David killing two hundred Philistines for their foreskins (ugh) resembles Samson killing thirty men for their clothing when his riddle was discovered (159). All rather horrible.

So why are these resonances about Samson surfacing now? Let's hold this question in mind.

Meanwhile, in our next story, Nabal is going to die of thirst but in an opposite way to Samson – his excessive drinking will bring on a medical emergency which leads to his death. He thought he was a strong man, Samson-like maybe, but he wasn't. However, we are getting ahead of ourselves.

יָרֵך
thigh

Back to Saul in the cave. We read that David and his men are positioned in the YaRKThe of the cave (160). NIV translates this as being far back in the cave, which helps make sense of the story. However, YRK means 'loin' or 'thigh'. One might say they were at the sides of the cave, YaRKThe being the plural form of YRK.

Let's pursue the idea of loins for a moment. In an earlier time, Abraham sent his servant off to find a wife for his son Isaac from among his relatives in the East. He made the servant swear an oath of loyalty, and this required the man putting his hand under Abraham's thigh – YRK (161). I understand this action to symbolise keeping faith with Abraham's offspring. That idea seems to be confirmed by the next occurrence of YRK. Jacob finds himself in a crisis, and to add to his problems, a strange visitor wrestles with him at the river Jabbok at night. We noted alliterative rootplay in that passage earlier in our study.

When the stranger is unable to overcome Jacob, he strikes him in the hollow of his thigh, his YRK (162). Whatever the result in terms of the wrestling, and Jacob was left limping through Peniel afterwards, I think that this action symbolised the mysterious assailant laying claim to Jacob's offspring. God's hand was going to be on the race that would spring from his loins.

Fast forward to David and his men in the loins of the cave. Is there any connection with these earlier stories?

Well yes. There's a struggle here too; Saul, the Lord's anointed, desperately trying to kill David, also the Lord's anointed. Despite all attempts by Saul to remove him, David is determined to keep faith with Saul and his descendants. Not only Jonathan, with whom he has made a covenant of loyalty, but with other descendants notably Mephibosheth, a crippled young man who is yet to come into the story, whose real name seems to have been Merib-baal (163). The use of the word YRK highlights David's unwavering loyalty to Saul and his descendants for me.

Oh dear. These thoughts have helped me see an aspect of the Samson connection. If we look forward into Two Samuel, David is going to end up victorious over all his enemies, but then he is going to fall over his affair with Bath Sheba, the wife of Uriah the Hittite. Not much faithfulness with Uriah's descendants there. And this point about the thighs of the cave. We wondered earlier whether there were hints of Saul's future demise at Apheq in the vocabulary used about him. Do we have a foreshadowing in the use of YRK here of David's fatal error over an attractive woman involving thighs?

When calling out after Saul, David asks why Saul would pursue a dead dog like him (164). CeLeB, dog, always makes me think of Caleb, as we discussed earlier, and Nabal, the next character in the story whom we have already met, is going to end up as a dead Calebite. A dead dog, practically. Surly Nabal is about as far removed from his upstanding ancestor as he could be. Let's move on to discuss links between the story of David and Saul in the cave with the encounter with Nabal.

Nabal

נֲבָל
Nabal

The name Nabal means fool; we are told this specifically by his cultured and good-looking wife Abigail (165). I find this extraordinary. Fancy being addressed as Fool, especially in a society where names were so important. Strange.

לחי
Lehi / to life

David greets Nabal with the word LHY – 'to life', in other words, your good health. These three letters also spell Lehi, Samson's place of thirst, encouraging us once again to consider a possible link between David and Samson (166). Incidentally, the musical Fiddler on the Roof contains a drinking song L'Hayim in praise of life and health, which is the same word. Friends of ours with a high regard for Israel even named their home L'Chaim, to the probable confusion of visitors and postmen.

נבל
Nabal / wine skin

Nabal knows about serious drinking. With a different pronunciation, NeBeL, his name means wine skin, as we noted earlier. The pompous wine skin will soon be punctured.

At this point, I want to pay tribute to someone I have never met. I don't even know his name, but what I was told was that in a talk to the Old Testament Study Group at Tyndale House Cambridge, the speaker alerted his listeners to the fact that the story about Nabal the fool comes sandwiched between two stories about Saul attempting to catch David but himself being caught out. Saul lost a piece of his cloak in the cave to David's stealthy approach in the earlier story, and he will lose his spear and water jug in a daring night time raid by David and Abishai in the following one.

Saul's response to David calling out from a distance about his spear and water jug is to confess that he has behaved stupidly – acted like a fool as one translation has it (167), and this confession of folly encourages us to see the three stories as a triptych. Saul is like Nabal, a big or great man (168). Physically in Saul's case, and as a man of property in Nabal's case. Like Nabal, Saul thought he could flick David away like a flea – the word comes in both the stories about David avoiding Saul (169), but like Nabal it's only a matter of time until Saul's life will be over, as David points out to Abishai, his accomplice in the night time raid (170).

By highlighting the similarity between adjacent stories that appear unconnected, the author of the paper opened my eyes to the possibility of other links between stories of a revealing kind which are not necessarily adjacent, as we have been investigating.

I intend shortly to try to trace details of his talk, but before I do I want to say this. As a result of to me unwise decisions by politicians, the pressure is on academics to publish as much as they can these days. Never mind if their work is really advancing the state of knowledge or not. It's daft really. I would rather have one good or outstanding paper than twenty mediocre ones.

It's already depressing to feel that after all one's efforts, the writing is hardly likely to be read by more than a handful of people. I have a happy memory of consulting a theological paper in German which was dated 1893 and was not to be found in the Cambridge University Library to my surprise, but which happened to be available in the basement of the library at Downside Abbey near Bath. The monks kindly allowed me access. When I had taken the bound volume down from the shelf and blown the dust off it, I found the pages had not been properly separated during the printing process and I needed to borrow a knife to part them. I was the first person to have looked at this learned tome, possibly in the entire country. Disappointing for the author.

But the point is that I did consult it, albeit ninety years after it had been published. In the case of the Nabal / folly paper on One Samuel, I did not even look at it; I came across it through hearsay only. The author's insight has stayed with me all these years and influenced the way I approach the text of the Hebrew Bible.

There. I have now managed to find the paper. It was the Tyndale Lecture for 1979, and it can be read freely online or downloaded (171). The author was Robert Gordon. Thank you Robert so much! You have no idea how helpful I have found your insight.

So take courage all you writers who feel that your efforts meet with little or no response. You never know what may happen in the future as a result of your endeavours. We all need to keep at it when we feel discouraged.

Now to some more matters arising from the story about Nabal.

David the outcast moved to the wilderness of Paran (172). This was where Hagar brought up Ishmael when they were outcasts, driven away by Abraham's wife Sarah (173). We will return to this passage shortly.

הי ו ת ם

while they were

In his message to Nabal, David says that his shepherds had no trouble from David's men 'while they were' in Carmel. The word is HYWThaM (174). I noticed the name of YWThaM or Jotham within it (underlined above), and turned up the story about him in Judges (175).

Abimelek, whose name means 'my father is king', murdered sixty-nine of his seventy brothers so that he would be the undisputed king of the people. However, Jotham the youngest son survived. It seems that the idea of kingship had been tried then, despite Gideon, Abimelek's father, stating clearly, "I will not rule over you, nor will my son rule over you, but the Lord will rule over you." The Shechemites made Abimelek king (176).

God did not approve, and he sent an evil spirit between Abimelek and the citizens of Shechem so that they would destroy each other, in response to Jotham's wish shouted from the top of mount Gerizim that just that would happen. Jotham himself immediately went on the run to get away from Abimelek (177). Note the irony in passing; mount Gerizim had been intended as the place for pronouncing the blessing, but here it became a scene of calling down a successful curse (178).

So the story of Jotham, the rightful 'king' on the run from a usurper, is one of Abimelek's botched attempt at kingship going wrong. A foretaste of things to come regarding Saul and David?

Note also that Shechem has entered the story once again. It was a place of treachery in Abimelek's day, both regarding Abimelek's brothers and the overturning of their father's insistence that there be no king. However, it turns out that it was also the place where Joshua and the people had renewed the covenant with the Lord after the conquest was completed some years before (179). Perhaps we should therefore refine our view of Shechem, and say that the reference to Saul's shoulders that we noted earlier, while speaking of the probability of treachery to come, also alerts us to the possibility of a strong union with the Lord in line with the covenant made by Joshua and the people. Which way will Saul go?

הַמִּתְפָּרְצִים

are breaking away from

Nabal is not impressed by David's request for provisions, and complains about servants who 'are breaking away from' their masters (180). The root meaning 'break away' is PRS or as we know him, Perez; he was the twin who broke out first from his mother's womb as a result of Judah's affair, the account of which reads like an awkward interpolation into the story about the seventeen year old Joseph (181).

Judah had moved away from his brothers and gone to Adullam. We read about David in the cave of Adullam recently. When he was born, little Perez was seen as a result of prostitution. Not a good start in life. However, despite being an outcast, it turned out that he was the boy whose descendants would eventually produce king David. That is presumably why the story of the birth of Perez was preserved.

So Perez turning up in this latter-day story about the unwanted David has a pleasing ring to it.

חֲגוֹר
Hagar / gird on

Reading on in our story, David was not at all pleased by Nabal's rejection. It was time for action. "Come on, men, gird on your swords," he commanded, so the men girded on their swords and David girded on his sword (182). The thrice repeated word for 'gird on' is HaGaR, reminding me of the outcast mother in the wilderness of Paran we mentioned earlier who narrowly escaped death along with her boy.

So we have three references to break-away people under a cloud – Jotham, Perez and Hagar mother of Ishmael all in a few verses couched in a story where Nabal is criticising David as being a slave that has broken away from his master. We know that it was not like that, but it raises the question of what people at the time would have thought. Why was David on the run? What has he done? Why was Saul seeking his life?

Our insights demonstrate that David has joined a league of unwanted men, outlaws even. Coincidence, or an instance of literary subtlety?

Nabal's wife Abigail hears of David and four hundred of his men on the march coming to get even with Nabal. She prepares gifts, loads them on donkeys, and sends them ahead of herself. This reminds me of Jacob seeking to placate vengeful Esau with his four hundred men after his life and death struggle at the Jabbok (183). Perhaps this is encouraging; David and Abigail are going to team up, so maybe in his struggle with God and man David may prevail ultimately like his ancestor had done.

When Abigail reaches David, she falls at his feet. In her speech, she mentions the men who serve at

David's feet (184). Two further mentions of feet in the following verses all combine to remind me of Saul relieving himself in the cave, covering his feet, as we mentioned earlier. Just in case we still have not got the point, David refers to Nabal's male servants not simply as men but as those that urinate against the wall (185). All this feels like an additional conscious attempt to link the episode in the cave to the account of Nabal to my mind.

I always feel sad that David took Abigail as his wife when I read this passage. He already had a wife, or even two. We observed the pain that Elqanah having two wives caused to Hannah at the start of our story. The rivalry with Peninah was nothing compared to the hatred among Jacob's children, born to four women. It's all a long way from the creation ordinance, that a man should leave his parents and become one with his wife. David's tendency to have a trickle of women is going to become a torrent in his son Solomon's life, leading to his loss of relationship with God and then to the breaking up of the nation in the next generation and onwards towards the eventual exile of the people. Grim foreshadowings indeed. But that's for another book (186).

I do wonder whether the links between Nabal's story and the previous cave scene are to alert us to this train of thought. We are increasingly aware of

Saul's impending downfall, but we are now becoming dimly conscious of David's forthcoming demise. Depressing.

נָבָל
Nabal / wine skin / lyre

There is one more possible wordplay involving Nabal's name. It turns out to have a third meaning as a musical instrument. Let's go with 'lyre'. It was one of the instruments being played by the 'band' of prophets that Saul met in his final encounter on his extraordinary day of meetings predicted by Samuel. Saul's immediate response was to prophesy in the power of the spirit (187).

We have already wondered whether the story of Nabal the man of property was prophetic. I'm also reminded of the end of the book of Deuteronomy, where God says that when the people eat their fill and thrive in the land flowing with milk and honey, they will turn to other gods, rejecting the Lord, and breaking his covenant (188). Nabal was eating his fill. He had no time for someone who was the Lord's anointed. He was perhaps a fulfilment of that prophecy.

I wonder. I'm really not sure about this. You may agree with me that this suggestion is perhaps somewhat NeBuLous. (I enjoyed that).

The Spear and the Water Jug

Jeshimon

The second incident of David's removal of personal objects from Saul – it's strange how things happen in twos in One Samuel – takes place near Jeshimon (189). The opening three letters of this word spell the name of David's father Jesse.

This might be considered accidental, but David has been referred to several times as being the son of Jesse. This was first made clear on Samuel's visit to Jesse's home to find the Lord's anointed, and secondly in the subsequent story of the killing of Goliath, when Saul asks Abner whose son the young man is, and learns that he is the son of Jesse (190).

However, there are more instances. Later on, at the time of the new moon festival, Saul asks Jonathan, "Why hasn't the son of Jesse come to the meal today?" He refers to David as being the son of Jesse twice more in his meal-time conversation with Jonathan (191).

Later, when Saul harangues his servants, he accuses them of aiding and abetting the son of Jesse. Doeg the head shepherd picks up the phrase and refers to David as being the son of Jesse in the same way (192). Then most recently, Nabal asks his servants in indignation "Who is this David? Who is this son of Jesse (193)?"

In short, David being the son of Jesse comes all over these chapters. It's almost like a refrain.

Now here it is again in the name Jeshimon.

לא אביתי
I was not willing

When David calls from the top of the hill across the valley to Saul, "I was not willing to raise my hand against the Lord's anointed", his turn of phrase included ABY which means 'my father' when taken on its own (194). Saul was David's father-in-law, as David was married to Saul's daughter Michal.

Saul refers to David as being his son four times in the two stories of removal of Saul's personal items. "Is that your voice, David my son?" (195). This too was correct; David was Saul's son-in-law.

I therefore note the role of close family from all these indications. This highlights the contrast between the two men. David's life will be preserved, despite his father-in-law Saul's many attempts upon it. Saul and his sons will go down, despite David's refusal to raise a hand against Saul his father-in-law. Faithfulness and treachery side by side in the intimacy of a family setting. Family feuds are always grim. Oh dear.

Have you noticed the importance of family in the Bible? When a new character is introduced, we often hear something about their ancestors. In the books of Chronicles, this tendency is taken about as far as it can go. What a contrast with modern Britain, where family ties have become so weak. Half of marriages fail, between a quarter and a half of viable pregnancies are terminated, maybe a third of our teenage girls self harm. I find the statistics so sickening that I barely want to write them down. It's dreadful. One Samuel all over again.

The Nocturnal Séance

דור   עין   דוד

Dor   Een / eye   David

We now come to what is perhaps the darkest moment in the Hebrew Bible. Saul seeks out the departed spirit of Samuel at night. The event takes place at 3YN DWR or Endor, the Spring at Dor (196),

3YN means 'eye' as well as 'spring'. Curious. There's generally a connection to be found when Hebrew words seem to have more than one meaning. In this instance, I wonder whether the glint in a person's eye was considered similar to the sparkle of light on a spring of flowing water.

דוד   דור
D W D   R W D
David   generation

DWR means generation. The word also looks very like David when written; D has a square corner, while R has a rounded corner. David is never far away from our thoughts.

Perhaps we can speculate a little on the meaning of the name. 'Generation Spring' comes most obviously to mind, or in the light of our conversation about fathers and sons a moment ago, 'Family Spring'. But is there also a hint of a gleam in David's eye in the name Endor? 'Eye of David'? Probably not, as I don't think of David in that way, but the thought did cross my mind. Saul's visit to Endor is the beginning of the end for him, which is sad and grim, but it is also David's big chance. Saul may soon be out of the picture, which could open up a better future for David than being part of the Philistine troops. A suggestion of light at the end of the tunnel.

Saul adopts a disguise by wrapping himself in a robe, to deceive the lady, who soon discovers the truth. She describes the apparition as a god coming up from the ground, looking like an old bearded man dressed in a cloak. (the root ZKN means 'old' and also 'bearded'). Saul immediately decides it is Samuel. I have the impression from the text that he does not see the figure himself but is reliant on the lady. Frankly the whole scene is all very weird.

I have a strong sense already that no good is going to come from the encounter. I have only ever heard bad things arise from a visit to a person that deals in fortune telling. There was a young lady once who was told, amongst other things, that she would die at the age of eighty-four. This was many years ahead at the time of telling, but as the decades passed and the date approached she became more and more troubled by the prediction. Bad news!

During the seven years when I was a curate in the church of England, I must have taken forty funerals or so. On one occasion, a mourner told me about the deceased in the bun-worry afterwards (lovely old-fashioned word) "he was always terrified of the snow, because he had been told he would die in the snow." The date was October the fourth, and there was no hint of any snow. His fear was groundless.

The mistake seems to be to allow yourself to believe what these people say. The effect is that of receiving a poisoned dart; seemingly innocuous to begin with but life-sapping in the end. (Remember Frodo's wound in Tolkein's *Lord of the Rings*?) The whole area is best avoided to my mind. Life has enough challenges as it is without adding more.

Saul clearly believed the prediction made about him, to the point where he even helped to bring it about. It's such a sad end to a life that had seemed so full of promise to begin with.

Why was God so unwilling to respond to Saul's request for guidance, we wonder? Perhaps it was a case of what Zechariah the prophet would point out to his hearers in a later day: "'When I called, they did not listen, so when they called, I did not listen' says the Lord of armies (197)."

I notice that Saul expected God to speak through dreams as well as through the Urim and prophets (198). He remained open to the spiritual realm all his life.

There are one or two points of vocabulary that link the episode at Endor to previous stories. The woman is concerned that her visitor is seeking her out to put her to death (199). This is what Saul has been trying to do to David of course. Saul's reassurance that no harm will come to her is sufficient for her, but David did not trust Saul's promise, hence his departure to Achish the Philistine king (200). Was the woman wise to trust Saul? In her case the promise stands firm, but not thanks to Saul, as he was no longer in the frame.

עָרֶךְ
your adversary

Samuel, whether supposed or real, explains to Saul that God is now his adversary – 3RK. This word is formed by 3R meaning 'adversary' with the suffix C or K turning it into 'your adversary' (201).

יְרֵךְ   קְרַע   יָדֶךָ   רֵעֲךָ
thigh   seize   your hand   your friend

It so happens that 3RK sounds like YRK, the word for 'thigh' that we discussed when David was in the 'sides' of the cave. Reading on we hear the spirit say that God has 'seized' – QR3 the kingdom from 'your hand' – YDK and given it to 'your friend' – R3K David. These words might be considered instances of rootplay highlighting the word 'thigh' (202). So are there other connections between our story at Endor and the incident in the cave?

By communing with nature in the dark interior of the cave Saul was putting his life in danger, but he did not know it. By communing with the departed spirit in the dark of night, Saul is again putting his life in danger, but this time he does know it, and the fact that he has put mediums and spiritists out of the land demonstrates that he is aware that what he is doing is wrong. What a numbskull. By communing with Bath Sheba, David will be playing with fire in his turn. Human beings, eh?

In both stories, Saul's kingly robe is involved. In the former, he loses a piece of it. Here he has dispensed with all of it, to deceive the lady, but to no effect. Samuel had said earlier that the torn hem of Saul's robe symbolised the tearing away of the kingship (203). In the cave, a larger portion of the robe had been cut off. Now Saul has laid aside his entire robe. His death is not far off.

נבהל   נבל

disturbed   Nabal

When the supposed Samuel has delivered his judgement, the woman sees that Saul is very NBHL – 'disturbed'. This word is Nabal with an extra H in the middle (204). Saul is in the same state as Nabal now. He has heard his death sentence, and it is as if he is paralysed like Nabal was. He has also been very foolish, like the prosperous farmer.

The woman tries to persuade Saul to eat and drink, and when he refuses his two servants 'break out' – PeReS against him (205). This was the word Nabal used earlier of servants breaking out against their master. In Nabal's case, it was a criticism of David and others like him. Here servants are once again breaking out against their master, but this time out of loyalty and to good effect.

זַבַ
sacrifice

Saul changes his mind at their urging, and eats the fatted calf that has been 'sacrificed' – ZeBaH for him, recalling the sacrifices of Eli and sons at Shiloh and the meal Saul enjoyed with Samuel at their first meeting where the root ZBH is employed (206). Whoever would have thought then that Saul, of whom there was none better in Israel, would turn out like this?

I also see possible links to Hannah way back at the start of our story. She refused to eat the sacrifice, sought the living God out of desperation, and the result was the birth of Samuel and other children; Saul fasted, sought the dead Samuel out of desperation, and the result was the death of his children. Hannah and Saul both cast themselves down full length, in her case in worship alongside her husband, and in Saul's case in terror (207). Note the contrast. Finally, Elqanah asked his wife why her heart was R33 – evil, following provocation from her rival Peninnah, and Saul's heart, also troubled by a rival, was filled with dread (208). Two deeply troubled hearts with very different outcomes.

Ziklag

We need now to return to the story about David, which wraps around Saul's encounter at Endor in a similar way to Saul's stories of pursuit wrapping round the account of Nabal. David settled in Ziklag, which king Achish gave him (209).

The name of this foreign town with its unfamiliar ring stands in contrast to the Israelite names we have encountered. These are generally to do with a family member linked to a quality, such as the priest who comes in our passage named Abiathar – 'The great one is my father', who was the son of Ahimelech – 'My brother is king' (210).

Sometimes the Israelites chose names of a similar construction involving the name of God 'EL' such as Elqanah – 'God acquires'.

אֵלִיָּהוּ   יהוה
Elijah   HWHY

If the tetragramaton YHWH, pronounced Yahweh and generally translated as 'The Lord', is used in a name, only two or three of the letters are employed, as in Elijah's name ELYHW – 'YHW is my god' or 'The Lord is my God'.

The people of that time seem to have had the feeling that the whole four letter name of God was not to be used in speech or writing. I wonder what that was about; I imagine it had to do with honouring God.

We didn't consider the meaning of Elqanah earlier. Perhaps we should have done. How is 'God acquires' going to be relevant in our story which seems to have been mainly about setbacks?

Now that David was living in Philistine territory, his daily activity was to slaughter a whole village or city and leave no survivor to tell Achish the truth, that David was not attacking Israel as Achish supposed, but rather her enemies (211). So much for Abigail's plea that David should avoid shedding innocent blood. His actions now copy those of Doeg regarding the people of Nob. How horrible. The day will come when David wants to build a temple to

God, and is told no because he is a man of blood (212). The temple is to be built by his son Solomon, whose very name suggests he will be a man of 'peace' – ShaLoM.

לשׁט	משׁפט	פלשׁתים
destroy	manner / judgement	Philistines

There may be some rootplay in our passage. David PShT – destroys villages. That's his manner of life, or as the text puts it his MiShPaT, his 'judgement'. This happens while he is with the PLiShTYM, the Philistines (213). Judgement on the Philistines and their allies. Perhaps David is becoming Philistinised? Philistinisation, a new concept and probably a new word but unfortunately too long for a game of Scrabble, even though it would just fit on the board which is fifteen letters wide.

The Philistine leaders refuse to have David fight alongside them, saying he may turn out to be a Satan in their midst – an adversary. Achish insists that David is as an angel of God (214). To my mind, these are the two possibilities regarding the 'god' that ascends from the earth in response to the medium at Endor. Is the mysterious apparition godly or demonic?

אוב   איבי   אבוא

| I come | enemies | medium |

There may even be a reference to the word for medium in the phrase where David asks Achish, "Why should I not come and fight the enemies of my lord the king (215)?" 'I come', 'enemies' and 'medium' are all constructed from the same letters.

I remain far from sure as to who the spirit being that Saul summoned was, and I have the impression from this rootplay that maybe this uncertainty was present in the mind of the author of these chapters too. Mystery.

There is also considerable use of the phrase 'in the eyes' in the passage. Achish declares to David that he is right in his eyes but not good in the eyes of his chiefs, so he is to go home in peace and avoid doing what is bad in the eyes of the chiefs. When David remonstrates, Achish repeats that David is good in his eyes, like an angel of God (216).

This phrase always reminds me of the closing chapters of the book of Judges when everyone did what was right in his own eyes and the national life careered sharply downhill into chaos (217). We have already considered its earlier use in One Samuel, but its fourfold use in just three verses here makes me wonder whether the author wants us to focus yet again on the similarity with the earlier time.

On that occasion, life was spiralling out of control so rapidly in the nation that was meant to be the people of God that it looked as if there would be no way back. Well, things are dire now as well. David the shepherd and anointed king of Israel is on the verge of leading his six hundred battle-hardened men into war against the very people he is meant to be shepherding with skilful hands, to quote the Psalmist (218).

Get out of that if you can, as they said to Houdini. Perhaps God can bring order out of chaos, like he did at the beginning of creation? Will there be light despite the darkness of the closing chapters of one Samuel? We will have to wait and see.

David and his men return to Ziklag on the third day to find that Amalekites have attacked his encampment and set fire to it. However, they have not killed the wives and children, like David and his men used to do, but carried them off instead. After a hairy moment when the men in their bitterness are considering stoning David, God hears David's urgent request, in contrast to Saul's experience, and tells him he will certainly succeed in a rescue mission.

In their pursuit, they find an exhausted Egyptian who has eaten nothing for three days. This recalls Saul at Endor, who had eaten nothing for a day, at pretty much the identical moment to the Egyptian if you compare the three day time frame (219). Like Saul, the Egyptian is revived with foot and drink, and leads David and his men to the Amalekites, who are dispatched in short measure. The wives and children are all rescued. David can breathe again.

Saul's chosen fast precedes disaster for Israel at the hand of her enemies. The Egyptian's imposed fast precedes victory over enemies for David's people, the hope of Israel. You couldn't make it up.

From Gibeah to Gilboa

So we come to the sad end of Saul. His life and that of his three sons comes to a conclusion on the battlefield, not with a bang but a whimper (220).

The names of the sons are perhaps worth mentioning. Jonathan means 'The Lord has given'. It uses three out of the four letters of the tetragrammaton. Abinadab means 'My father is noble' (is he?) and Malchishua means 'My king cries out for help' (yes he does) or perhaps 'My king is salvation' (not this time).

We know next to nothing about Abinadab and Malchishua, but Jonathan has been a key player, along with his armour bearer, when the two of them acting alone achieved a great victory over the Philistines as we saw earlier.

Not any more. Saul and his armour bearer recall the earlier scene for us. (David had been an armour bearer for Saul at one time, but he has since been replaced (221)).

At that time, the armour bearer's response to Jonathan was, "Do what's in your heart; I am with you according to your heart (222)."

Jonathan's heart was full of faith in God, but Saul's heart is filled with dread in complete contrast. His armour bearer wants to respond to the noble king Saul crying out for help, to pick up the thoughts from his sons' names, but is instructed instead to do what's in Saul's heart, which means killing him. It puts the armour bearer in an impossible position.

Another point linking our story with that of Jonathan and his armour bearer is that in both passages, the concern is with 'these uncircumcised people', the Philistines (223).

In addition, both stories mention not eating food. Saul was famished when he visited the woman, as we saw. Jonathan was hungry, and his eating of the honey almost cost him his life, because Saul had imposed a fast on his army until the enemies were routed. Jonathan knew nothing about the food ban but Saul's men did – they were exhausted with hunger themselves as a result.

Jonathan eating honey he found by chance reminds me of Samson and the bees that made honey in the dead lion. 'Out of the strong came something to eat' worked for Samson then, and for Jonathan in the wood, but there is no honey available for Saul now, in what had been promised to be the land flowing with milk and honey (224). The flow has dried up.

God giving victory to invading enemies in response to the disobedience of his people is a key theme of this part of the Bible, most notably in the Book of Judges. Things have gone badly wrong in the nation and its king by the time we reach Gilboa. It's going to happen again.

הַמּוֹרִים   הַמֹּרִים

the archers   asses

There may be another link back to Saul's earlier story. His first action on being introduced to us was the search for his father's asses – AThWNTh. Here,

Saul is hard pressed by the archers – HaMWRYM, (literally 'shooters' of the bow (225)). The first letter of the word, Ha, is the definite article in Hebrew, and MWRYM are shooters. The word comes twice.

The word HaMWRYM is very similar to the alternative word for asses or donkeys – HaMWRYM, but this time spelt with a letter Heth rather than a letter He. The two letters are almost identical. You have to look very closely to see the difference. The similarity is close enough for me to have read the word 'asses' by mistake before realising it was actually a reference to the archers.

My confusion, or a deliberate ploy? Am I being invited to recall the young Saul of earlier days?

$$ויחל$$

from חול and חלל

whirl   begin

The use of the word WYHL is interesting. It seems here to be from the root HWL meaning to 'whirl', 'dance' or 'writhe' – in pain in this instance (226). The word 'contort' springs to mind. But YHL also relates to the root HLL, one of whose meanings is 'to begin'. So in reading that Saul 'contorted' from the onslaught of the 'archers', the idea of the 'asses' in the 'beginning' flashes through one's mind momentarily, it seems to me. Saul who was once keen to find missing asses has now been found by them in the form of archers; they have returned to bite him.

The rout is complete. Israel retreats beyond the Jordan. What a disaster.

The Philistines only realise that Saul and his sons are dead the following day. They take the bodies home in glee.

גבע   גלבע
Gibeah   Gilboa

Mount Gilboa where Saul died was obviously lifted above the plain, as was Gibeah, Saul's home, which means hill. The similarity in place names also reminds me of Saul's origin.

The Philistines cut off Saul's head, the leader of Israel, in a grim reprise of what had happened to Goliath's head, who was the chief Philistine. Chief in the sense not only of being leader but also a head taller than anybody else, like Saul. The executions accompanied Israel in victory through the boldness of David, and in defeat through the fear of Saul.

It's worth pondering some rootplay in the earlier narrative that I missed on our way through the book. Easily done. Let's observe the QaL and KaL sounds in the Hebrew.

קלעו	בילקוט	בכלי	חלקי	מקלו
his sling	in a receptacle	his equipment	smooth	his staff

קלל	מקלות	ילך	הלך
he made light	light things	he walked	walking

And David took *his staff* in his hand and chose five *smooth* stones from the valley and placed them in *his equipment* of shepherds, *in a receptacle* and with *his sling* in his hand drew near the *walking* Philistine who *walked* to meet him... (Goliath) said, "Am I a *dog* that you come to me with *light things*" (i.e. sticks and stones) and *he made light* of David (227).

I wonder if the purpose of the rootplay, if you agree with me that it is present, is to draw our attention to the 'making light', which NIV translates with the word 'curse', the final word in the series.

קלל   עלל   חלל

make light make sport   pierce

I also notice that In the account of Saul's death, the root HLL meaning 'pierce', i.e. kill in verses one and eight, and the use of the root 3LL mid way between them in verse four, where Saul's concern is that the enemy will 'make sport' of him if they get the chance, both sound similar to the root QLL, to 'make light' of, or to 'curse'.

If you agree, then our thought process linking the death of Saul with the death of Goliath may carry more weight. Saul has made light of the living God by his attitude and actions. He has put himself under the same curse as Goliath had done.

The four royal corpses are hung up in Beth Shan. The strong men of Jabesh Gilead are having none of it; they rescue the bodies and give them a decent send-off. They remember how Saul had delivered them from Nahash the serpent in the early days. Well done you men of valour. Nice that the book ends on a strong note.

The Riddle of One Samuel

We've reached the end of our meander through the text, our journey of discovery. I've enjoyed it very much; I hope you have too.

It's time to take stock. Do all these proposed literary devices actually help me to make better sense of the book than if I had simply read it through in an English translation?

I think they do. Let's take our most recent example.

Gibeah, Saul's mount of origin, was similar to Gilboa, Saul's mount of departure. The archers – HaMORim reminded me of the asses in the earlier story. The armour bearer for the father and the earlier one for the son were both with their masters heart and soul. Noting all this, I found the end of Saul's story linked to its beginning in several ways.

As I reflect on this, I find further points of interest. Saul had not wanted the kingship, and when it was offered his comment was that he was a nobody, from the smallest and most insignificant clan of the people of Israel (228). Samuel's response was to anoint him with oil, and get him going on hearing from God during his remarkable day of initiation into prophecy.

When the time came to step forward, Saul showed signs of reluctance or uncertainty. Do you remember him hiding among the baggage when the moment of declaration came? He was hardly a keen candidate for the job.

In contrast, by the time of his death, Saul was desperate to hang onto the kingship, for himself and his sons. However, the reality was that he had become a nobody once more. The Israelites may have grasped that he had died, and responded accordingly, but the Philistines did not even know that they had killed him. They only found it out when they were stripping the abandoned bodies on the battle field next day (229). My impression is that the archers which had looked so threatening to Saul were attacking the enemy army in general, not trying to focus their energy on its leader.

While thinking about this, I realised a connection with Eli too, further back where our story began. Eli, his two sons and his daughter-in-law all died on the same day, one of battle with the Philistines at Apheq, four family members in all, matching the death of Saul and his three sons at Apheq. The ark was captured; all that was left then was poor little baby Ichabod whose name we translated 'Where is the Glory'.

The glory has certainly departed now. Moreover, the battle is described as being KBD – heavy, the very word we commented on in the account of Eli and the temple at Shiloh, culminating in the birth of Ichabod or Ai – KBD (230). A chance occurrence? It's hard to be sure, as the word is used frequently in the Hebrew Bible.

Who knows where the ark is by now? It is no longer of central concern. The hope and glory of the nation rest on David instead, the Lord's anointed. Some hope: he is as good as a prisoner, having become a Philistine mercenary distrusted by the five lords, with his life in danger from the hands of his own men as well. The glory has departed from Israel once more. We are left wondering, will it ever return, and if so, how?

Perhaps it is time to recall Joseph in prison once again. We thought of him several times before. His story is a reminder that all is not lost even in the darkest days.

I submit that these thoughts have come to me as a result of noticing the verbal subtlety in its varying forms. They are encouraging me to wrestle with the central issues of the book. This makes paying attention to the possible plays on words worthwhile to my mind.

גִּבְעָה   גִּלְבֹּעַ
Gibeah   Gilboa

Finally, here is an additional thought about wordplay. When you saw the heading at the beginning of the previous section, from Gibeah to Gilboa, did you pay any more than passing interest to it? I expect it just seemed to you to be a reasonable heading for a section that aimed to see Saul's life in the round. A pleasing title with something of a ring to it.

A friend of mine who is in book publishing once told me that a title is a tease. Its aim is to entice the reader. I have never read the book *Zen and the Art of Motorcycle Maintenance*, but I do think that the title is brilliant in this regard. It's my number one book title to date for rousing my interest.

Nowadays, there are further ploys available to publishers. The front cover design of a paperback provides a first encounter with a book, and it needs to be sufficiently appealing to get the potential reader to turn the book over and read the back cover blurb, which itself needs to be well written. Glowing words of praise from well-known people dotted around on the front and back covers and repeated inside the volume before the title page may help too.

If all these elements pull together successfully, the book has a higher chance of being bought and read.

None of these modern marketing techniques were available for the authors of the ancient world. The only means at their disposal was the text. So it seems reasonable that there might have been enticements within it to encourage readers to delve deeper. Something to elicit a smile, stimulate interest or provoke thought. Or so it seems to me. I think plays on words and literary subtlety may have performed this role in at least some instances.

So given all that we have discovered and discussed, what is the book about?

To me, it's all about impending disaster. Eli and his sons ruin the sacrificial system of the temple and pay the price. Several of my proposed literary devices recalled the creation and the garden of Eden before the fall; we are a world away from the perfection of those times now. Samuel and his sons bring the role of the judge to an untimely end. The people ask for a king, which God allows with reluctance, and the prophetic role that was intended, whereby the king heard from God and led the people accordingly, becomes so badly damaged that the first king ends up in witchcraft, trying to control God, in a complete reversal of what was wanted.

Do you remember Samuel saying that rebellion was as the sin of witchcraft? Saul will choose to go full tilt down that route in the end. We missed that insight as we read through. Now we can appreciate the irony of Samuel, so keen on prophecy, prophesying accurately about Saul's witchcraft in the future without realising what he was saying; the root QSM, to 'summon a spirit', comes in both passages (231).

Even God himself seems to be in a bind at the end of our story, as we suggested earlier. The plan of salvation is not going well at all. Reminders of the lives of Abraham, Jacob, Joseph, Moses and Joshua have helped keep God's overall plan in our minds as we have read. If Barry Webb's attractive proposal that Samson's chaotic love life stands for the people of Israel's obsession with foreign gods is accepted, then the links between the name of Samuel, Saul and Samson with which we began our study can be seen to serve a similar purpose (232). Like Samson before them, the central characters in One Samuel also comment on Israel's rebellious attitude to God, which the prophet Ezekiel would one day refer to explicitly (233).

However, all is not lost. David is the ace up God's sleeve. Perhaps he will be Israel's true strong man.

How will he turn out? Don't miss the next compelling instalment...

I observe that much of this summary of the book could have been gleaned without taking any note of my proposed literary devices. No matter, as I also note that the literary subtlety, if correctly identified, tends to underline the understanding of the book that we would have had without reference to wordplay. The two approaches are not in competition with each other.

My parents used to enjoy solving the crossword in the Daily Telegraph each day in the 1970s. I recall my mum once saying to me that on some days, she could arrive at the answers with ease. She decided it was because she was in tune with the person who had created that day's puzzle, and that there must be other puzzle makers to whom she did not relate so well.

The question in my mind over my proposals in this book is whether I have tuned in well to the mind behind the text in the way my mum found she was able to do. I think so, but I simply don't know. So interesting.

Perhaps it is premature to end our study here without pressing on into Two Samuel, but at the age of seventy-two and with my medical history, I feel that every new day is a bonus. Better to get this volume finished and available than wake up dead one morning with it locked away inaccessibly in my computer. So we will finish there.

I might have a go at Two Samuel if life, brains and wits allow, or someone else might care to do it. After all, I suspect that the division of the books of Samuel into two was for practical rather than theological reasons; two shorter scrolls would be easier to manage than one longer one. But I do want to end this volume by commending attention to possible plays on words in the Hebrew text of the Bible. I think they are worth pursuing, with the aim of gaining deeper understanding of the concerns of the text. Unearthing them is also good fun.

I don't doubt that there are more instances of literary devices in One Samuel which I have missed. Richard Bicknell's insight that the name of Samuel emerges from the phrase 'his name was Elqanah' when the words are run together suggests a line of enquiry: create a text without spaces, an easy task in these days of computers, and learn to read it, as this is what early readers had to do. Who knows what might surface?

Happy hunting as you look for your own insights.

Whoops

Will this book ever be completed?

This is what happened. I decided I ought to read through the Hebrew text once again, to make sure I was happy with what I had written, and see if there were any obvious wordplays I had missed.

רחב
to be large / Rahab

I only got as far as the opening verse of Hannah's prayer in chapter two when I bumped into RaHaB (234). The word means 'be large', and comes in the phrase 'my mouth is large over my enemies', or if you like, 'my mouth boasts over my enemies'.

Fine. But wasn't Rahab the name of the dubious tavern keeper in Jericho who hid the spies on the roof and then sent them off on their way safely (235)? If my system of noting possible references to names is along the right lines, should I consider her?

At first glimpse, I could see no possible connection between Rahab and Hannah, apart from the fact that they were both women. I tussled with the notion for twenty-four hours and then gave it up, wondering whether I should ditch my entire thesis, as here was a counter example which simply did not fit. As you can observe, I am not totally confident in what I am presenting. Some of my insights feel stronger to me than others. Maybe all of them are no more than a will-o-the-wisp.

But then, I reflected further. Joshua's two spies spent the night on Rahab's roof. Didn't Saul and his young man spend the night on the roof when they met Samuel (236)? We are told that twice, and I recall wondering briefly when I read that passage earlier why the roof detail was repeated, before shrugging my shoulders and moving on.

Where might this thought lead us? After all, Saul and the young man were hardly spies. However, like Joshua's men, they were sent safely on their way (237).

הרגלים

---
ones on foot

The word for the two investigators in Joshua's day was MRaGLYM, which literally means ones on 'foot' – RGL (238). They were spying out the land, true, but the word 'spies' feels rather Cold War, so let's call them 'scouts'.

Saul and his young man were also scouting, in their case for lost animals. Interesting.

Then I came up with this comparison of the two events.

Joshua, God's chosen leader and saviour of the people, sent scouts to see what was happening in the land. They ended up on the roof. The lady of dubious morals, to put it politely, revealed to them that the whole nation was in dread of the Israelites. She gave them instructions as to the way they should take. When her message got back to Joshua, it proved influential in the success of the conquest and invasion of Canaan, despite the efforts of the king of Jericho to find and eliminate the two men.

Saul and his fellow scout wanted to know what was happening and ended up on the roof, but the message they received was that Saul was the national saviour for whom the whole nation was waiting and they should forget the animals. Saul was also sent on his way. He was instantly caught up in all the excitement, practically becoming a prophet on the spot, and was confirmed as the choice of God and of Samuel; there was no one better among the people than him. The people were thrilled to be having a messiah, an anointed king.

In Joshua's time, the message and its consequences led to life and blessing for the nation. In Samuel's day, the message, initially so promising, turned out to be hopelessly wrong and led to disaster for the nation; by the end of the book, Philistines were living in what had been Israelite towns in a reversal of the invasion and conquest (239).

Comparing the two sets of scouts sleeping on the roof has been helpful to me in noting the contrast. I'm pleased to have spotted the name Rahab in Hannah's speech as I did.

This brings me back once again to the central puzzle of the book; how could God and Samuel have got things so spectacularly wrong? Why did God choose someone who looked like an ideal choice but was going to go so badly off the rails when it came to the point?

Alright, despite his great gift of hearing accurately from God, Samuel the 'seer' was capable of defective vision, as Rashi pointed out: when Samuel was looking at Eliab, Jesse's older son, he was sure this would be God's chosen one, but God said no. Samuel was looking at the appearance, not the heart (240). So Samuel was capable of getting things wrong. But God knows the future – we know as much from Samuel's prophecies about Saul's extraordinary day of self-discovery with their pin-point accuracy. Couldn't God have chosen David to begin with and by-passed the wretched Saul altogether?

Or is it possible that God wanted the first king to fail? He had never desired a king in the first place. "The Lord works everything out for his own ends — even the wicked for a day of disaster" wrote Solomon. Hosea commented "I gave them a king in my anger and in my fury I took him away (241)."

Then again, how could God overlook Samuel's appalling sons?

I am reminded of a time at school when a teacher told us about a man who was an expert in the Arctic. Every year, he explained, the explorer would travel there to learn more, and when he came back he knew less than when he went. At the time, this appraisal seemed an impossible mystery to me, but now I can see what the teacher meant. It sums up my feeling about the book of One Samuel. For all my insights, I feel as puzzled about the book as ever, if not more so.

Let's stop there. I feel I have discovered pockets of gold, but rather than trying to mine it all myself, word needs to be got out, so that others can look for themselves. Maybe there can be a gold rush as in the American mid west. I believe the only people to profit from that endeavour in the end were the ones that supplied picks, shovels and boots, but never mind that; let's hope that the miners had fun and made a lot of friends as well as some enemies. And found some gold too.

I'm realistic. It probably won't happen. People may conclude that I'm talking nonsense, and not for the first time; some of my books have sold less than ten copies. But maybe a dozen or so people will read this and find there is some value in it, and the insights and my way of reading the text will do us all good in the end. I hope so. Unearthing the plays on words has certainly benefitted me.

They have also given me an appetite to see what other discoveries are around the corner. Maybe I will push on into Two Samuel after all. Who knows?

That's it, finally. Time to put my pen down. Thank you for your attention.

List of Proposed Devices

Within One Samuel, 34 involve names and 15 do not. The remaining 9 devices are from elsewhere in the Hebrew bible.

Notes

BDB is *The New Brown Driver Briggs Gesenius Hebrew Aramaic English Lexicon*, Associated Publishers and Authors, Lafayette, Indiana, 1981.

Rashi is quoted from the helpful website chabad.org/library/bible_cdo/aid/15831/jewish/Chapter-1.htm/showrashi/true.

1. David Pennant, *The Significance of Rootplay, Leading Words and Thematic Links in the Book of Judges*, Council of National Academic Awards 1989. Available at www.academia.edu.
2. Judges 4:18.
3. Judges 13:3-5, 1 Samuel 1:2 & 11.
4. Isaac Kalimi, *Metathesis in the Hebrew Bible*, Hendrickson, Massachusetts, 2018, subtitled *Wordplay as a Literary and Exegetical* Device, was reviewed by Ingrid Faro in The Catholic Biblical Quarterly, 2021. Scott B. Noegel, *"Wordplay" in Ancient Near Eastern Texts*, Ancient Near East Monograph 26, SBL Press, Atlanta, 2021 addresses the lack of a complete taxonomy and consistent vocabulary in the field of wordplay in a most valuable and thorough treatment containing many references to recent scholarship in the field. For a brief but helpful introduction to the

subject, see Kurt Helm, "Wordplay" in Tremper Longman III ed., *Dictionary of the Old Testament: Wisdom, Poetry and Writings*, Downers Grove IV, 2008, pages 925 – 929.

5. V. Phillips Long, *The Reign and Rejection of King Saul. A Case for Literary and Theological Coherence*, SBL Dissertation Series 118, Scholars Press, Georgia, 1989, pages 28-9. On 1 Samuel 14:28-29, he commented 'Jonathan's rootplay, converting curse (ARR) to brightening (AWR) adds to the developing contrast between him and his father' (page 120). This I find more helpful. See Kalimi *op. cit.* pages 29-30.

6. Elizabeth H. P. Backfish, *Hebrew Wordplay and Septuagint Translation Technique in the Fourth Book of the* Psalter, Library of Biblical Studies, T & T Clark, 2019, page 81, writing about Psalm 101:3. Cf. Kalimi *op. cit.* page 160 "Literary-stylistic metatheses add aesthetic beauty and rhetorical interest to a wide range of biblical phrases and passages."

7. Scott B. Noegel ed., *Puns and Pundits: Word Play in the Hebrew Bible and Ancient Near Eastern Literature*, CDL Press, Bethesda Maryland, 2018, page 204.

8. *Puns and Pundits* page 222.

9. *Puns and Pundits* page 230.

10. *Puns and Pundits* page 248.

11. Moshe Garsiel, *The First Book of Samuel. A Literary Study of Comparative Structures, Analogies and Parallels*, Revivim Publishing House, Hamaudil Street, 4 Ramath Gan, 1983 (translated from Hebrew), page 21 – 22 on 1 Samuel 14:24 and Judges 11:30-31. See also his *Biblical Names: A Literary Study of Midrashic Name Derivations and Puns*, Bar-Llan University Press, 1991.

12. Rabbi Bahya Ben Asher, *Commentary on the Pentateuch*, (thirteenth century), helpfully quoted as the opening line of Scott B. Noegel, *Janus Parallelism in the Book of Job*, JSOTS 223, Sheffield, 1996. A word with two meanings, one looking forward and one looking back, is an instance of Janus Parallelism: see his pages 29 – 30.

13. Genesis 35:18.

14. Genesis 45:24.

15. Ishbosheth son of Saul, who appears in 2 Samuel 2:8 to 4:12, is named as Eshbaal son of Saul in 1 Chronicles 8:23 and 9:39.

16. Genesis 25:26.

17. Genesis 25:33.

18. Genesis 32:28.

19. Genesis chapters 29 – 39.

20. Numbers 14:24.

21. 1 Kings 18:39.
22. 2 Kings 19:37.
23. Judges chapters 6 – 8.
24. Judges chapter 3.
25. Daniel chapter 3.
26. J. Chotzner, *Hebrew Humour and Other Essays,* Luzac and co, London, 1905, page 1 on Job 42:14. The word suggests black eye-liner. See 2 Kings 9:30 & Jeremiah 4:20. (BDB 806c).
27. A suggestion of Annelies Hiscock. Zippy is also sometimes used as a first name as a contraction of Moses' wife Zipporah.
28. 1 Samuel chapter 1.
29. Judges chapter 13.
30. Judges 13:3, 1 Samuel 1:4.
31. 1 Samuel 1:20.
32. 1 Samuel 1:28.
33. 1 Samuel 10:14-16.
34. 1 Samuel 14:50.
35. 1 Samuel 2:14.
36. 1 Samuel 1:24.
37. Genesis 30:24.
38. 1 Samuel 3:6 & 8.
39. 1 Samuel 12:11. Rashi reckoned that Bedan in this list means Samson, because he was 'in Dan', or in the tribe of Dan.
40. 1 Samuel 7:13-14.
41. 1 Samuel 3:15.

42. Judges 11:34.
43. 1 Samuel 1:7 house of the Lord, 1:9 temple of the Lord, 1:24 house of the Lord, 2:22 tent of meeting, 3:3 temple of the Lord, 3:15 house of the Lord.
44. Genesis 14:14 and 15:2.
45. 1 Samuel 2:5.
46. 1 Samuel 2:21.
47. 1 Samuel 16:20.
48. Jeremiah 25:26 and 51:41.
49. I Kings 11:40, 14:25.
50. 1 Samuel 14:13 & 29.
51. Isaiah 5:7.
52. Amos 8:1-2.
53. Jeremiah 1:11-12.
54. Numbers 12:6-8.
55. Isaiah 1:1.
56. Nehemiah 8:8.
57. Judges 14:12f.
58. Phrase of Roger Forster of the Ichthus Fellowship in the early 1970s.
59. I Kings 10:1.
60. Psalms 49:4 and 78:2.
61. Psalm 147:13.
62. Genesis 32:22-24.
63. One possibility is that the word PNYM – 'face' may be in mind. The boys had no sense of

seeking the Lord's face. I failed to note which commentator has suggested this – apologies.

64. Numbers 25:6-13; Psalm 106:30-31.
65. 1 Samuel 2:27-36.
66. 1 Samuel 2:36. This fact has also been noted previously.
67. 1 Samuel 2:29 & 32.
68. 1 Samuel 2:29. Compare Genesis 1:1.
69. 1 Samuel 3:13 'judge' and 2:31 for 'hack'. Gideon's story comes in Judges 6 – 7.
70. 1 Samuel 4:21-22.
71. 1 Samuel 2:29.
72. 1 Samuel 4:21.
73. 1 Samuel 5:6 & 7 (two mentions).
74. 1 Samuel 5:11.
75. 1 Samuel 6:6.
76. Ezekiel 1:4-28, chapter ten and 43:1-5.
77. 1 Samuel 2:30.
78. 1 Samuel 3:19. Have you noticed the hint about our future in space in Psalm eight? Exciting. See About the Author at the end of this book.
79. 1 Samuel 5:6, 9 and 6:5.
80. 1 Samuel 6:7.
81. Judges 3:12.
82. Judges 3:23, 24 & 25.
83. 1 Samuel 2.39.
84. Judges 3.22.

85. 1 Samuel 28:24.

86. Judges 3:19, 1 Samuel 3:11f. The word DBR is admittedly common.

87. Judges 3:25-6.

88. James 5:5.

89. Judges 5:26.

90. 1 Samuel 5:11.

91. 1 Samuel 6:12.

92. Judges 17:6, 18:1, 19:1 and 21:25.

93. Judges 18:12f.

94. Judges 18:31, 1 Samuel 1:3 etc.

95. Judges 19:14-15.

96. Judges 19:13, 1 Samuel 7:17, 8:4.

97. Judges 21:8-10, 1 Samuel 11:1.

98. Judges 19:29, 1 Samuel 11:7.

99. 1 Samuel 11:2, Judges 16:21.

100. 1 Samuel 6:14.

101. Judges 21:21.

102. 1 Samuel 8:3.

103. Proverbs 11:1 for example.

104. Malachi 3:6.

105. 1 Samuel 9:8.

106. 1 Samuel 9:7 – 9, Genesis chapter 42.

107. Genesis chapter 40.

108. 1 Samuel 9:7.

109. An example of Scott Noegel's Janus Parallelism maybe? See note 12 above. I did not find other examples in Judges or One

Samuel. See the discussion on 1 Samuel 9:7 in David Toshio Tsumura, *The First Book of Samuel*, Eerdmans, Grand Rapids / Cambridge, 2007 for other views.

110.1 Samuel 8:10, 10:22, 12:17 & 19.

111.1 Samuel 9:2, 10:23.

112.1 Samuel 17:4.

113.1 Samuel 17:23.

114.Genesis chapter 34.

115.1 Samuel 10:9.

116.1 Samuel 11:1.

117.Genesis 2:25 – 3:1.

118.1 Samuel 19:24.

119.Numbers 21:8.

120.1 Kings 18:4.

121.1 Samuel 14:1, four times in 4, 6, 8, 23.

122.1 Samuel 14:11.

123.1 Samuel 13:3, 7, 19, 14:11 & 21.

124.1 Samuel 14:8.

125.1 Samuel 13:7.

126.1 Samuel 14:6.

127.1 Samuel 14:23.

128.1 Samuel 13:14.

129.1 Samuel 15:28.

130.Prophecytoday.uk, online comment in September 2023. See Proverbs 28:13.

131.As in Psalm 9:20/21. See 1 Samuel 1:11 and BDB page 432b.

132. 1 Samuel chapter nine and 16:9.

133. 1 Samuel 13:15.

134. Judges 7:7.

135. 1 Samuel 14:2.

136. 1 Samuel 13:12.

137. 1 Samuel 29:1 and 4:1.

138. Genesis 3:4.

139. 1 Samuel 15:32. See BDB page 588d.

140. BDB 726c.

141. 1 Samuel 16:12 & 17.42.

142. 1 Samuel 17:4, 23; 21:9-10. The title Goliath of Gath also comes in 2 Samuel 21:19-20 & 1 Chronicles 20:5-6. David ends up at Gath in 1 Samuel 27:2.

143. 1 Samuel 17:44.

144. 1 Samuel 17:5-6.

145. 1 Samuel 17:44, Genesis 2:19-20 & 9:2.

146. 1 Samuel 17:32.

147. 1 Samuel 22:18-19.

148. 1 Samuel 25:22, 27:9.

149. 1 Samuel 9:9 & 11.

150. 1 Samuel 21:7.

151. J. Weingreen, *A Practical Grammar for Classical Hebrew*, 2nd edition, Clarendon Press, Oxford, 1959, page 3.

152. 1 Samuel 9:5.

153. 1 Samuel 9:11-13, Exodus 2:16-17.

154. Rashi on 1 Samuel 9:13.

155.1 Samuel 24:4.

156.Judges 15:9-20, Exodus chapter 17 & Numbers 20:10

157.1 Samuel 18:17-27, Judges 15:2, recalling not only the Timnite girls but Jacob's experience over Leah and Rachel, Genesis 29:16f.

158.1 Samuel 18:25, Judges 16:9.

159.1 Samuel 18:27, Judges 14:19.

160.1 Samuel 24:3.

161.Genesis 24:2.

162.Genesis 32:26.

163.1 Chronicles 8:34.

164.1 Samuel 24:15.

165.1 Samuel 25:25.

166.1 Samuel 25:6, Judges 15:17. LHY means 'jawbone', which was Samson's improvised weapon for dealing with the Philistines.

167.1 Samuel 26:21, New International Version.

168.1 Samuel 25:2.

169.1 Samuel 24:14, 26:20.

170.1 Samuel 26:10.

171.Tyndale Bulletin vol. 31, 1980, *David's Rise and Saul's Demise: Narrative Analogy in 1 Samuel 24 – 26*. Visit tyndalebulletin.org.

172.1 Samuel 25:1. NIV omits.

173.Genesis 21:21.

174.1 Samuel 25:7.

175.Judges chapter 9.

176.Judges 8:23, 9:6.

177.Judges 9:7, 20-22.

178.Deuteronomy 27:12.

179.Joshua 24:15.

180.1 Samuel 25:10.

181.Genesis chapter 38.

182.1 Samuel 25:13.

183.Genesis 32:6.

184.1 Samuel 25:24 & 27.

185.1 Samuel 25:34.

186.I have always thought of Solomon's advice to his son in the early chapters of Proverbs about the dangers of the loose woman and the adulteress to be the wise advice of someone who had avoided temptation. Now I wonder whether his words are the heartfelt outpouring of an older man who had made mistakes in his relations with women and regretted it.

187.1 Samuel 10:5.

188.Deuteronomy 31:20.

189.1 Samuel 26:1.

190.1 Samuel 16:1, 17:58.

191.1 Samuel 20:27, 30 & 31.

192.1 Samuel 22:7, 8, 9 & 13.

193.1 Samuel 25:10.

194.1 Samuel 26:23.

195.1 Samuel 24:16-17, 26:17, 21 & 25.

196. 1 Samuel 28:7.

197. Zechariah 7:13.

198. 1 Samuel 28:6.

199. 1 Samuel 28:9.

200. 1 Samuel 27:1.

201. 1 Samuel 28:16.

202. 1 Samuel 28:16-17.

203. 1 Samuel 15:27.

204. 1 Samuel 28:21.

205. 1 Samuel 28:23.

206. 1 Samuel 1:21, 9:12 etc.

207. 1 Samuel 1:19, 28:20.

208. 1 Samuel 1:8, 28:5 & 20.

209. 1 Samuel 27:6.

210. 1 Samuel 30:7.

211. 1 Samuel 27:9 – 11.

212. 1 Chronicles 22:6 – 8.

213. 1 Samuel 27:8 – 11.

214. 1 Samuel 29:4 & 9.

215. 1 Samuel 29:8.

216. 1 Samuel 29:6 – 9.

217. Judges 17:6 & 21:25.

218. Psalm 78:72.

219. 1 Samuel 30:11-12. See 30:1.

220. 1 Samuel chapter 31.

221. 1 Samuel 16:21.

222. 1 Samuel 14:7.

223. 1 Samuel 14:6 & 31:4.

224.Exodus 3:8 and another dozen places.

225.1 Samuel 31:3.

226.1 Samuel 31:3, see BDB page 297a and 320a2.

227.1 Samuel 17:40-43.

228.1 Samuel 9:21.

229.1 Samuel 31:8.

230.1 Samuel 31:3.

231.1 Samuel 15:23 & 28:8.

232.Barry G. Webb, *Theme in the Book of Judges: A Literary Study of the Book in its Finished Form*, PhD Dissertation, University of Sheffield, 1985 and *The Book of Judges*, Journal of the Study of the Old Testament Supplementary Study 46, Sheffield, 1987.

233. Ezekiel 2:4 – 8 etc.

234.1 Samuel 2:1.

235.Joshua 2:1.

236.Joshua 2:6, 1 Samuel 9:25 - 26.

237.Joshua 2:21, 1 Samuel 9:26.

238.Joshua 2:1.

239.1 Samuel 31:7.

240.Rashi on 1 Samuel 16:7.

241.Proverbs 16:4, Hosea 13:11.

About the Author

Of most relevance is my book *What's the Difference Between D and R? My Journey into Biblical Hebrew*, Silver Lining Books, Woking, 2022. For those who are interested in the language and might be tempted to dip in a toe.

My other eight books fall into two classes. Three are about what a Christian church might look like and my desire to see one emerge in the UK during my lifetime.

The remaining five are what looks like science fiction. These arise from my reading of Psalm eight. The works of God's hands are seen there as being under humanity's feet, i.e. we are in charge of them – animals, birds etc. But what about the moon and stars – are they under our feet as well? Why yes, because they are the work of God's fingers, which if you think about it is the same as the work of God's hands. So scripture hints that the galaxy and beyond is waiting for us to colonise it, to my mind. I can hardly wait. I was very excited when I first read that.

So rather than science fiction, I call my writing future prediction. I am confident that the big gun which I write about in *The Garden of the Galaxy* will be built one day. I also hope that there will be a

Bruce Winter around (an obscure *Piano Teacher*) to save the universe from catastrophe due to technology getting out of control. Today's world is too like the chaos of One Samuel for my liking.

Details are on my website with links to Amazon where the books can be bought. I try to keep prices as low as I can – I make my money from teaching piano.

I also compose music, mostly for piano, which hardly anybody plays other than me. They would rather play Mozart and Beethoven, and I for one don't blame them.

I live in Woking UK with my wife and grown up son. I also have a married daughter and three grandchildren. Nice.

Appendix

"New-fangled jangling bangles for my angel" whispered Danny intimately as he handed over the booty. "Cheep and cheerful for my girl. A new angle." The delicate music from the string quartet on the other side of the restaurant created just the right atmosphere.

"Aw, thanks" murmured Molly, for whom square bangles were a novelty. "Now you know how to please a gel."

Danny frowned briefly. Why did she have to pronounce now as if it rhymed with bear? If only Molly could get the hang of how to speak proper, like Angela used to...

-oOo-

Comment. Danny may claim to be over Angela, but as 'angl' sounds seem to creep into his conversation with his new girl friend at every opportunity, perhaps he isn't. His turns of phrase betray his state of mind.

Printed in Great Britain
by Amazon

34465241R00089